THE ESSENCE OF ZEN ■■

THE ESSENCE OF
ZEN

SEKKEI HARADA

TRANSLATED AND EDITED BY
DAIGAKU RUMMÉ

WISDOM PUBLICATIONS • BOSTON

Wisdom Publications
199 Elm Street
Somerville MA 02144 USA
www.wisdompubs.org

Library of Congress Cataloging-in-Publication Data
Harada, Sekkei, 1926-
  [Zen. English]
  The essence of Zen / Sekkei Harada ; translated and edited by Daigaku
Rummé.
     p. cm.
  Includes bibliographical references and index.
  ISBN 0-86171-533-0 (pbk. : alk. paper)
  1. Zen Buddhism. 2. Sotoshu. I. Rummé, Daigaku, 1950- II. Title.
  BQ9265.4.H3713 2008
  294.3'927—dc22
                            2007036425
12 11 10 09 08
5 4 3 2 1

Cover design by Rick Snizik. Interior design by Gopa & Ted2, Inc.
Set in Trump Mediaeval 9.75/16.5.

CONTENTS

PART III
AWAKENING TO THE TRUE SELF

PART IV
ELEMENTS IN THE PRACTICE OF ZEN

This is a translation of Sekkei Harada's book *Zazen* (Zen Meditation), which was published in 1993 and is now in its fifth printing. It consists of a collection of relatively easy-to-understand talks on Zen that were given to Westerners to explain the timeless concepts of Buddhism and the principles of Zen.

Many sorts of people can benefit from reading this book. For those who are curious about Zen Buddhism but have never read about it, the principles of Zen are clearly explained. For those who have an intellectual understanding of Zen but have never actually practiced zazen, again it provides a clear explanation of the method of sitting in zazen and why it is necessary to go beyond intellectual understanding. For those who have been practicing zazen for many years but feel that something is lacking in their practice, Harada gives advice and encouragement. For those who have attained a measure of comfort and ease in their practice, but still wonder if it is possible for them to attain—in Zen Master Dogen's words—"the culmination of totally realized enlightenment," Harada emphatically says, "Yes, it is certainly possible." In short, this is a book for all people—regardless of age, experience, gender, race, or creed—who seek the Dharma, the natural principles of things, and keenly desire to know their true Self.

For me, this book is the warm body and breath of the buddhas and ancestors who have transmitted the Dharma in centuries past, akin to the records of past enlightened Zen masters. Open the book to any section and the underlying message of Harada Roshi's teaching is quickly apparent. In order to attain true peace of mind, it is imperative that we forget the small self—the grasping, demanding "me" that is never satisfied. This isn't an easy task, but it is a necessary one. If it is accomplished, there will be a transformation, in that we directly realize the Self that is without beginning or end, the Self that transcends time and space and is one with all things. This is Harada's message, as clear and sharp as a diamond, and is one that people of both East and West are longing to hear. More and more people are attracted to Buddhism because of such teachings as the law of causality, the fundamental equality of all beings, and the necessity of always living in the present moment. I think people are also very much attracted to the Zen teaching that we must liberate ourselves by our own efforts. By introducing Harada's teaching to a wider audience, it is my fervent wish that this book will help foster the true Dharma in the West.

To the many people who have assisted me in preparing this translation, I would like to express my deepest gratitude. May all beings awaken to their innate freedom!

Daigaku Rummé

INTRODUCTION

Many people think Zen is something difficult. This is a misunderstanding. The Chinese character used for "Zen" means "to demonstrate simplicity" or "to point at oneness." As this character implies, Zen is an extremely clear and concise teaching.

Who is it that creates this labyrinth where the body-mind is entangled in troubles and complications to such an extent that it is impossible to move? Regardless of whether you live in the East or West, it is you yourself. The cause is nothing other than ignorance of the true Self.

"Do you know yourself?" "Who are you?" If you were asked these questions, how would you respond? In answer to the earnest desire to know the essence of oneself, which means to meet the true Self, Zen offers the search for that Self, and it can be undertaken anywhere at any time.

You may resolve to do zazen, but almost immediately your resolve may weaken when you remember the hardships recounted in Zen literature or by other practitioners of zazen. You reinforce the negative aspects. To further weaken your resolve, you remember other difficulties, such as the fierce pain in the legs and back that often accompanies zazen practice, the rigorous stillness. Imagining what zazen is like, you quickly conclude that you will never be able to persist and that you will perhaps only hinder those who are more earnest. Many people lose heart this way.

Accordingly, this book is written in part for those who want to practice zazen but have never actually gotten as far as doing it. The book gives a simple and concrete explanation of the theory and principles of Zen, as well as its reality and essence.

Zen can also be expressed with the words "the Dharma," "the Way," or "the Self." Why? The reason is that the existence of all things on the planet Earth is the Dharma. All things come into existence through conditions, and they disappear because of conditions. This is what we call "the law of causality." There is absolutely no possibility of the intervention of the ego-self in this law. We can say that all things on Earth are completely equal because of this law. This is the Buddhadharma.

Zen Master Dogen said that Buddhists should not discuss or debate whether a teaching is right or wrong, correct or incorrect, good or bad. Nor should we inquire into the depth or shallowness of the contents of the teachings. The only thing that is important is whether a person is now truly practicing in accordance with the law of causality, in other words, with the Way of the buddhas and enlightened ones who transmitted the Dharma.

Speaking of the near future, I think that as long as there is no coexistence or mutual support among people, mankind will become extinct in the twenty-first century. As long as there is only one Earth, the situation in any country has implications for the whole world. As the saying goes, "If a person sneezes in the Amazon basin, someone in Tokyo catches a cold." Similarly, if one country is selfish in the way it thinks or in its scientific research, this can bring about the destruction of both human beings and Earth itself. The sufferings and deluding passions of human beings—namely, greed, anger, and ignorance—cannot be halted by reason or education. Only by awakening to the law of causality is it possible to stop them.

As you know, Zen and the Buddhadharma developed in the different cultures of India, China, Korea, and Japan. The different forms that appeared from the varied cultural backgrounds attest to the functioning of the law of causality. Unfortunately, Zen practice itself has fallen into self-centered habits. This is a Zen sickness (the sickness of thinking you are not sick), which is difficult to be aware of. It can cause great harm, and at present it is a sickness that is widespread in the Zen world, both in Japan and abroad. It causes me constant anxiety.

Many people who are not Japanese are doing Zen practice. While overcoming the problems of language, environment, diet, and so on, they continue to practice earnestly. During retreats, held abroad, as well as at practice centers In Japan, I have given the Dharma talks which form the basis of this book, concerning aspects of zazen and the Dharma. I have spoken in familiar, concrete terms about the essence of Zen. Much of the repetition has been eliminated in this edition, yet the careful reader may find some remains. I hope the reader will overlook, or even appreciate, these repetitions.

Finally, I would like to express my heartfelt gratitude to all those who helped with the English translation and production of this book.

Sekkei Harada
Hosshin-ji
Japan

PART I
DOGEN'S FUKAN-ZAZENGI
AND COMMENTARY

The *Fukan-zazengi* is arguably the single most cherished text in the Soto Zen sect. It is recited in Soto Zen monasteries each evening at the end of regularly scheduled zazen. It was written by Zen Master Dogen on his return to Japan from China in 1227.

THE *FUKAN-ZAZENGI* A UNIVERSAL RECOMMENDATION FOR ZAZEN

Now, when you seek the Way, you find it to be universal and complete. How, then, can it be contingent upon practice and enlightenment? The Dharma vehicle is free and unrestricted. What need is there for concentrated effort? Indeed, the whole body of reality is far beyond the world's dust. Who can believe in a means to brush it clean?

The Way is complete and present right where you are. What is the use, then, of practice? And yet, if there is the slightest difference between you and the Way, the separation will be greater than that between heaven and earth. If the least like or dislike arises, the mind is lost in confusion.

Even if you are proud of your understanding and think you are richly endowed with enlightenment and have glimpsed the wisdom that pervades all things; even if you think you have attained the Way, clarified the mind, and gained the power to touch the heavens, you are still only wandering about the frontiers of enlightenment. In fact, you have almost lost the Way of total liberation.

You must take note of the fact that even Shakyamuni Buddha had to sit in zazen for six years. The influence of those six years of upright sitting is still apparent. Also, Bodhidharma's transmission of the Buddhadharma and the fame of his nine years of practicing zazen facing a wall are celebrated to this day. The ancient sages were this diligent in their practice, so how can people today dispense with the practice of zazen?

You should therefore cease from practice based on intellectual understanding and the pursuit of words and letters. Learn the backward step that turns the light inward to illuminate the Self. Body and mind will drop away by themselves, and the essential Self will be manifest. If you wish to attain "suchness," practice "suchness" immediately.

For zazen, a quiet room is best. Eat and drink moderately. Give up all deluding relationships and set everything aside. Do not think of good or bad, right or wrong. Do not interfere with the workings of the mind, nor try to control the movements of your thoughts. Give up the idea of becoming a buddha. Zazen has nothing whatsoever to do with whether you are sitting upright or lying down.

Usually a thick square mat is placed on the floor where you sit and a round cushion put on top of it. Sit either in the full- or half-lotus position. In the full-lotus position, first place your right foot on your left thigh and your left foot on your right thigh. In the half-lotus, you simply put your left foot on your right thigh. Your clothing should be loose, but neat. Then place your right hand, palm up, on your leg and your left hand, palm up, on your right palm, with the tips of the thumbs lightly touching. Sit upright, leaning neither to the left nor to the right, neither forward nor backward. Be sure your ears are in line with your shoulders and your nose is in line with your navel. Your tongue should be placed against the roof of your mouth, with lips and teeth firmly closed. Your eyes should always remain open. *Breathe gently through your nose. Having adjusted your posture, take a deep breath. Sway your body to the left and right, then settle into a steady, immobile position, sitting like a mountain. Think of not thinking. How is this done? By leaving thinking as-it-is. This is the essential art of zazen.*

The zazen I speak of is not "step-by-step, learning Zen." It is simply the Dharma gate of comfort and ease. It is the culmination of totally realized enlightenment. It is the manifestation of ultimate reality. Traps and snares can never interfere with it. If you attain this, you are like a dragon that has reached water or a tiger that reclines on a mountain. The true Dharma then appears of itself, and you will be free of dullness and distraction.

When you rise from sitting, stand up slowly and calmly. Do not rise abruptly.

Through the power of zazen it is possible to transcend delusion and enlightenment and attain the ability to die while sitting or standing. However, it is impossible for our discriminating mind to understand how the buddhas and enlightened ones bring about enlightenment through the opportunity provided by a finger, a pole, a needle, or a mallet. Or how they have transmitted the Way with a fly whisk, a fist, a staff, or a shout. Neither can it be fully understood through supernatural powers. These actions are beyond the dualistic realm of subjective and objective. Is it not a principle that precedes knowledge and perceptions?

Therefore, no distinction should be made between whether a person is clever or stupid, superior or inferior. When you practice single-mindedly, that in itself is truly the practice of the Way. Practice and realization are naturally undefiled. Making an effort to attain the Way is itself the manifestation of the Way in your daily life.

All people throughout the world are without doubt equally imprinted with buddha-nature. However, without the practice of zazen, the true nature and function of a person will not be manifested. You should therefore devote yourself exclusively to and be completely absorbed in the practice of zazen. Although it is said that there are as many minds as there are people, all people should practice the Way, which is nothing other than the study of the Self. There is no reason to forsake the place you sit at home and go aimlessly off to the dusty regions of other countries. If you make one false step, you stray from the Way that lies directly before you.

You have already been blessed with a human form, which is vital, so do not use your time in vain. You are endowed with the essential functioning of the Way of Buddha, so why pursue worthless pleasures, which are like sparks from a flint stone? Our bodies are like dew on the grass. Our lives are like a flash of lightning, gone in an instant, vanished in a moment.

Honored practitioners of Zen, do not be afraid of the real dragon (zazen) or spend a long time touching only one part of the elephant. Devote yourselves to the Way, which points directly to the absolute. Respect those who have gone beyond all learning and have nothing left to do. Be in accord with the enlightenment of the buddhas and succeed to the samadhi of the enlightened ones who have transmitted the Dharma. Practice constantly in this manner and you are assured of becoming like them. The treasure house will open of itself, and you will be able to use it at will.

AN EXPLANATION OF THE TITLE

In the present world, explanation, rather than the actual condition or the thing itself, fulfills the needs of most people. As this does not inconvenience most people in their social life, they don't feel the need to know the true essence of things. They are stuck in this condition of ignorance, and consequently neglect to inquire into what is real. Changing our perspective and looking at this matter from the dimension of perception or the world of consciousness, the essence of things does not lie within the category of understanding or not understanding. What we perceive can only be either the past or the future. The central question must be what is "now," the point that divides past from future. But these days the thorough investigation of this question is completely forgotten. In the present moment, or "now," there is neither time, place, nor separation. There is truly nothing. This is the world where things arise and disappear because of causes and conditions. We could call this condition *"buddha-nature,"* or *"Dharma-dhatu"* (the true nature of things), or *"Buddha."* It would also be all right to call it *"God,"* or *"God-nature,"* or *"the Truth."* This is what we call *"now."* The objective of Zen practice is to give proof of this, to actualize it as your own thing.

We are living within buddha-nature. Our life itself is buddha-nature. Our life is practice and enlightenment, and because of that I would like you to understand that essentially the true Self is the self that is not subject to circumstances. This means that the moment "now" is not something that can be imported. Even though I have come here to speak today, "now" is not something that can be exported, either. Regardless of when or where, of whether a person is from the West or East, North or South, is an ordained priest or a lay person, young or old, man or woman, each person possesses "now."

"All things possess buddha-nature." Since each person possesses it completely, anyone can realize it if they set out to do so, and this is the meaning of the title, *Fukan-zazengi.* "*Fukan*" means "a universal recommendation." This does not mean attaining something new. Since you already have it, if you practice zazen you will certainly realize it. Zen Master Dogen points out that zazen is a universal teaching, one that should be recommended to all people far and wide. The Chinese character for "*gi*" stands for "significance," the true meaning of zazen. At the same time this work is a wonderfully detailed explanation about the posture for zazen and other points to keep in mind.

As indicated by the expression "*zazen is zazen,*" zazen is not something to understand, nor is it something not to understand. Zazen is beyond the realm of knowing zazen, or not knowing it, or knowing it just a little. Nor is it a condition where zazen deepens. "*Zazen is zazen*" and that is all there is to it. In the beginning, since some of you cannot fully understand that "*zazen is zazen,*" it is necessary to depend on various forms. But in actual fact, "*zazen is zazen.*" There isn't the slightest gap where the ego-self can slip in.

Another way this can be expressed is "without moving one speck of dirt, without disturbing a single phenomenon." This means that "as-it-is" is the "Mind of Great Peace." The central aim in Zen practice is to realize this "Mind of Great Peace" in the condition right now, both in the physical and mental realms. It means realizing that we must not look elsewhere.

As this is something that is difficult to believe even if you sincerely wish to believe it, this is expressed in Buddhism in the teaching of "the world of innumerable teachings." The number of these mysteries is said to be 10^{66}, a figure so large we cannot even imagine it. But if there are any people here who have some extra time, please try to calculate that number while you are sitting.

At this point I would like to caution you with regard to a way of thinking about zazen in which it is easy to be mistaken. In Zen it is said "no dependence on words and letters; a special transmission outside the teachings." Consequently, many people often think that it is best not to listen to too much talking. However, in order to attain the Dharma, first you must understand the teaching. Understanding the teaching alone is not enough to help us realize the Dharma, but listening to the teaching in order to find the right direction is a very important process through which you must pass.

COMMENTARY 1
YOU ARE ALREADY WITHIN THE WAY

"Now, when you seek the Way,
you find it to be universal and complete."
In these opening words, "seek" means that you must seek until you have clarified that "zazen is zazen." "Seek until you truly understand" is the meaning of the first phrase. "Now" means that from this moment on is the starting point for the proper way to look.

The "Way" refers to the "Way of Buddha," to "everyday mind is the Way." It is every aspect of our life. The only difference between someone who has realized this and someone who has not is whether the ego-self intervenes or not. Before your opinions arise, you are already one with each thing. Therefore, whenever, wherever, and whatever thoughts arise, we already are right in the middle of the Way, no matter what we are doing. We are people of the Way. We are in the midst of the result, we are people living in the midst of the results.

In another work by Zen Master Dogen, *Gakudo-yojinshu* (Guidelines for Buddhist Practice), there is an important section in connection with our search for the Way. Here is the passage.

First, you must believe that you are already within the Way.
You must believe that you are free of delusion, illusory

thoughts, confused ideas, increase and decrease, and mistaken understanding. Believing in this manner, clarify the Way and practice accordingly. This is the essence of studying the Way.

As I said earlier, we are already within the Way, so there is no delusion, there are no illusory thoughts, no confused ideas, no increase or decrease, and no mistaken understanding. We are free of these things. Usually we would say just the opposite—we think we are deluded with illusory thoughts, confused ideas, increase and decrease, and mistaken understanding, but in Buddhist practice we are already separate from these things. The above passage asks us to believe this as a first step and then to enter the Way.

These words were written by Dogen after his liberation, after he had "cast off body and mind." In our daily life, as I just said, delusion, illusion, and confused ideas are a fact; they are an unmistakable reality for people. To simply accept this fact, this reality as-it-is, is the first step in practice. It is the first guideline in Buddhist practice.

These five things—delusion, illusory thoughts, confused ideas, increase and decrease, and mistaken understanding—are what we usually refer to as the deluding passions. For bodhisattvas, these five delusions, these realities, are enlightenment, but for an ordinary person these five aspects of enlightenment are deluding passions. Depending on whether the ego-self is forgotten or not, these realities, as-they-are, become either enlightenment or illusions. The difference is that profound.

"You find [the Way] to be universal and complete" means that the Way has neither beginning nor end. There is no source of the Way. When you consider this, examine it in the light of the Zen expression "before your mother and father were born." In other words, where were you before your parents were born into this world?

"Universal and complete" means there are no rough corners, so that conflicts do not arise in any situation. It is impossible for friction to arise because essentially all is one. This means that the Way is all-pervading and completely free of restrictions. Dogen described this as "flexible mind." He said, "While I was practicing with Zen Master Nyojo, body and mind were cast off. In other words, 'soft, flexible mind' was attained." Regardless of the environment, a soft, flexible mind isn't rough or angular. It is the mind that has the freedom to be one with each thing. This is conveyed by "universal and complete."

"How, then, can it be contingent upon practice and enlightenment?"

We are already in the middle of the Way. We are already in the midst of Truth. There is no need, then, for any means or procedures, for practice or liberation, for enlightenment or kensho. These are all completely unnecessary. Simply to leave things as they are, forgetting the ego-self, that is the objective, the ultimate aim of practice.

One thing I would like to warn you about is what I have just said is an explanation from the standpoint of the Dharma, of how it is within the Dharma. But it is not so easy from the standpoint of human beings. You are making a great effort and undergoing considerable pain because you are not free of the ego-self. The ego-self consciousness is extremely tenacious in this way. I would like to caution you again and again not simply to listen to the explanation of how it is within the Dharma. Please don't simply accept an explanation of it.

"The Dharma vehicle is free and unrestricted.
What need is there for concentrated effort?"

"The Dharma vehicle" is the means for giving life to and using the Way. How is it used? You can think of it like a boat in which all things are carried to the other shore. "What need is there for concentrated effort?" This is to forget yourself ("me") by earnestly being each thing. That in itself is all that is required. Why, then, is it necessary to spend time concentrating on practice?

I sometimes speak of zazen of the body, speech, and thought. Zazen of the body is the form of zazen we are presently sitting in. It is the condition of zazen *samadhi*. Practice samadhi to the extent that there isn't the least margin for thought to enter. Zazen of speech is the sutra chanting we did this morning—just chanting the Heart Sutra and the "Four Bodhisattva Vows" is enough. Zazen of thought includes miscellaneous ideas and various other thoughts such as making plans. Zazen of the body, speech, and thought all take place separately from the consciousness of the ego-self. The Dharma vehicle functions actively in this way.

"Indeed, the whole body of reality
is far beyond the world's dust."
All the phenomena of the world that we perceive and observe are the Dharma and the Way itself. This is "the whole body of reality." Naturally, this means that there isn't the slightest possibility that dirt and dust, such as the deluding passions or enlightenment, delusion or realization, can enter.

"Who can believe in a means to brush it clean?"
As there is no dust or dirt, then there is no need for any cleaning. At this point I would like to relate an anecdote concerning Daiman Konin, the Fifth Ancestor in China after Bodhidharma.

In order to determine his successor, Daiman Konin arranged to give a test to the monks on the true Self. Initially, a monk named Jinshu gave the following answer: "Our condition is like a mirror. We must always clean the mirror, otherwise it will naturally become cloudy.

Constantly make an effort to keep it clean; never let it become dusty."

In response to this, Daikan Eno, another monk practicing with Daiman Konin, wrote: "Essentially there is nothing. Where can dust or dirt collect?" "Essentially there is nothing" means that fundamentally all things arise because of the law of causation and consequently have no substance. As there is no substance, dust and dirt—in other words, the deluding passions and enlightenment—cannot collect anywhere. This is how he answered the test question. I think it is clear to all of you which one passed the test. Of course, it was Daikan Eno, known as Huineng in Chinese.

However, if we have not heard of the Buddhist teaching and were to think of practice in the usually accepted sense, it would be easier for us to accept the answer of Jinshu, "Constantly make an effort to keep the mirror clean; never let it become dusty." This seems to be the correct way to practice, but it is clearly mistaken. These two viewpoints are as far apart as heaven and earth.

"The Way is complete and present right where you are.
What is the use, then, of practice?"
"Right where you are" is here, right now. *Now. Now. Now.* It means residing peacefully here right now. It isn't good to look for the Way elsewhere than right now. Since the Way is always right here, essentially there is no need for shikantaza, koan practice, or following the breath. Summing up once again, "right here" can also be expressed in other ways, such as "peacefully dwelling within the law of causality." Other than that, there is no way to practice. If you can live like that, then there is no need to take even one step in the direction of practice.

This passage is about the condition right now and the condition of practice. These words were written from the perspective of someone who has attained the Dharma. From the point of view of the Dharma, there is no doubt that it is this way. But it isn't like that for people. Regardless of how much you know, the deluding passions (greed, anger, and ignorance) or enlightenment always accompany you. Consequently, the actual state of your life will be one of suffering.

Human beings experience a whole range of emotional and rational states, including joy, anger, sadness, understanding, and not understanding. These are all part of the Dharma or the Way. We can freely feel these things, freely think these things. What other freedom beyond this are you looking for? I would really like you to believe that in our present condition we are endowed with the Dharma in this way.

During the forty-nine years that Shakyamuni Buddha expounded the Dharma, he never once said, "Believe in me." Rather he always said, "Believe in the Dharma. Believe in yourself." This is something you must believe resolutely. If you don't, the objective of your practice will not be clear. It is because you cannot completely believe that the practice of Zen is the study of the Self that you begin to look for the Dharma in the reasoning or teachings of Buddhism. Or you look somewhere else and are likely to go running off in the opposite direction. This seems to be your present condition.

The practice of Amida Butsu, or Amitabha, is widespread in Japan. I think many of you know that this involves chanting "*Namu Amida Butsu*" while prostrating oneself. In Zen Buddhism, a person who chants "*Namu Amida Butsu*" is already Amida Butsu. The object toward which prostrations are made, namely, Amida Butsu, and the person making the prostrations are one.

This next part is important. If you have made the resolution to believe, then it isn't good for the belief to remain. To believe means that there is someone ("you") who is believing. In other words, if something is truly believed in, then the belief must disappear. I would like you to understand clearly that you must let go of that which is believed in. The condition of pure belief is absolute. It is a condition where doubts and belief in a dualistic sense have disappeared. Belief and doubt or belief and disbelief are, in the end, the ideas of people. The condition where belief and doubt have disappeared is what we call "the Dharma," or "the Way," or "now."

There is a metaphor that conveys how difficult this is. It is likened to the immense improbability of a needle sinking to the bottom of the ocean and a silk thread coming down from heaven and passing through the eye of that needle.

COMMENTARY 2
GIVING UP THE EGO-SELF

From the viewpoint of the Dharma, we are essentially freedom itself. We are already liberated, a completely free body. But from the viewpoint of the ego-self, it is not like this at all. All sorts of restrictions arise because of the ego-self. Let us continue with the text.

"And yet, if there is the slightest difference
between you and the Way, the separation will be
greater than that between heaven and earth."
If the ego-self is perceived even to the slightest degree, the more you practice, the farther away you will be from the Way, from the Dharma, and from Zen. You will be farther and farther away from things.

"If the least like or dislike arises, the mind is lost in confusion."
It is because we don't know that the Way is essentially one that we show anger if we don't like something and drown in greed if we do like something. This condition is expressed in the words "if the least like or dislike arises."

"The mind is lost in confusion" refers to loss and gain or love and hate, this thing and that, good and bad. This means to see one thing as two. These two things then clash and fall into the realm of fighting devils, or *asuras*. It comes to the point that we even doubt the significance of our existence as human beings. This happens because we haven't clarified the nature of our real mind, of our true Self, or of the Truth. As I often say, delusion is seeing one thing as two. It is the suffering of dividing and comparing. Enlightenment means to realize that while things are separate, essentially all is one.

From this point on in the *Fukan-zazengi*, Dogen writes about several precautions to take concerning the way to practice. He does this in order to correct mistakes that arise in practice so we can move in the right direction. In any case, the primary objective is to forget the ego-self.

Each day we chant a short verse called "The Four Bodhisattva Vows." The first vow is to take all beings from the side of delusion over to the side of enlightenment. In order to accomplish this, the second vow is to eliminate all deluding passions, however inexhaustible. The third vow is to study all Dharma teachings, however numerous they may be. These are the Dharma teachings of Shakyamuni Buddha, the so-called 84,000 gates of the Dharma. Lastly, we vow to attain the unsurpassable Way of Buddha. This is the vow we make to clarify the Way, in other words, the effort we promise to make to understand the true Self.

We chant these vows again and again so that our practice doesn't end simply in our own self-satisfaction.

"Even if you are proud of your understanding
and think you are richly endowed with enlightenment
and have glimpsed the wisdom that pervades all things;"
Regardless of how wonderfully you can explain Buddhism and zazen,

and no matter how much you have learned from others about enlightenment and emptiness, if it isn't truly your own, it is nothing. Just saying the word "fire" doesn't burn your mouth, and just thinking of eating doesn't fill your stomach. What you learn from others is not enough.

Many people say things like, "I had an experience of forgetting myself, but it is no longer like that now." However, the problem is the condition right now. Past experience is not the problem. This isn't a matter of simply getting a glimpse of something like the Dharma or a feeling of what it is like to forget the ego-self.

Long ago, a Zen monk forgot himself on seeing a flower. In the same way, Kyogen cast off body and mind on hearing a sound. Some people have developed a great sickness because on hearing such stories they match their own experience with the experiences of people from the past. They strongly imagine that their condition is the same and become attached to this, even though it is they themselves who have created it.

In connection with the words "richly endowed with enlightenment" I might mention a priest from long ago named Daie, who said, "I've had eighteen great enlightenments and more small ones than I can count." What does this mean? All of them, whether big or small were false; they were not genuine. Satori isn't something that happens twice. It only happens once. In other words, it isn't an experience.

When we take a bath, we use a cloth to wash ourselves. After we have finished, we wring the cloth until there is no more water left. After a while more water can be wrung out of the cloth. Even if we repeat this again and again, it is difficult to wring all the water out. Enlightenment must be like a cloth that has been wrung completely dry.

For that reason both Shakyamuni Buddha and Bodhidharma underwent much pain and suffering doing zazen. The message here is that

practice should not end at a mere "glimpse of wisdom," or after forgetting the self many times. Casting off body and mind needs to be
done only once. In the same way, if one koan is truly resolved, then
it must be possible to resolve all the others.

"[E]ven if you think you have attained the Way,
clarified the mind, and gained the power to touch the heavens,
you are still only wandering about the frontiers of enlightenment.
In fact, you have almost lost the Way of total liberation."
This is "the power to touch the heavens" that a person imagines he
has by clarifying the Way, of having had kensho. Regardless of how
real this condition may seem, the mind, in fact, is scattered. In real
life, it will be of no use.

If you only get a glimpse of a room through a doorway, you know
nothing of what is actually inside it. In this way it can only end as a
grand fantasy for you. To say, "This is it!" will not then have any
meaning. Some people refer derisively to this kind of understanding
as being like a person who has himself certified his own qualification
as a physician. To truly understand—to really know or actually see—
is "not knowing." True wisdom is "knowing, but no perception of
that knowing remaining."

Earlier, the words "proud of your understanding" appeared. To be
proud means to feel better than someone else. You must perceive
someone else in order to feel proud. To be proud vis-à-vis another person is to perceive an object simply to feel proud. Your ideas have not
yet truly fallen away. This is an area that you must look into and
examine.

At some point in practice, you may find yourself perplexed, up
against "the silver mountain, the iron wall." Please don't use gim-
micks to try to break down this wall. The only way for great enlightenment to take place is to *be* "the silver mountain, the iron wall"

that is standing in your way. I would like you to exert yourselves even more. Don't hold back as you continue sitting.

It is possible to forget the self at any time or place. With regard to the way of zazen, there is absolutely no correlation with the length of a person's experience. To forget the ego-self is something that can certainly be done by anyone, regardless of how long or deep their experience is. In one way it is an advantage to have little experience in zazen and little knowledge about Zen. The reason is that if you know little about the theory or teaching of Zen, you are not always comparing what you know with your present condition. On the other hand, the more experience and knowledge you have of Zen the more likely it is that, without being aware of it, you will check the condition of your zazen with what you know.

"You must take note of the fact that even Shakyamuni Buddha had to sit in zazen for six years. The influence of those six years of upright sitting is still apparent. Also, Bodhidharma's transmission of the Buddhadharma and the fame of his nine years of practicing zazen facing a wall are celebrated to this day. The ancient sages were this diligent in their practice, so how can people today dispense with the practice of zazen?"
Here Dogen begins to warn us against being negligent in our practice of zazen. "You must take note" is a way of reminding us that Shakyamuni Buddha sat six years and Bodhidharma sat nine years. This is most essential in our present age.

"You should therefore cease from practice based on intellectual understanding and the pursuit of words and letters."
You must not think that you can find Zen or enlightenment within the records left by Shakyamuni Buddha, Bodhidharma, or the other

enlightened ones who have transmitted the Dharma. You must remember as you practice that Zen practice involves "no dependence on words and letters. It is a special transmission outside the teachings." "The pursuit of words and letters" refers to the realm of consciousness. It means that no matter how many sutras and commentaries you have read, or how many talks on the records of the buddhas and enlightened ones you have heard, all this takes place within the realm of consciousness. You never leave the realm of consciousness.

"Learn the backward step that turns the light inward to illuminate the Self."

How should we go about forgetting the ego-self? When perceiving—when you see or hear and so on—turn each thing back to yourself. This is "the backward step that turns the light inward." Then you may ask, "Who is it that sees? Who is it that hears?" By pursuing and studying this, the division between the thing seeing and the thing seen will disappear. This means that when you see, do it completely, and when you hear, do it thoroughly.

Those of you who are doing shikantaza are given the specific instruction to imagine yourself temporarily as a mirror. Neither the mirror itself that reflects an image nor the image reflected in the mirror is aware of what is happening. You are told to sit like a mirror in this way. But the strange thing is that people habitually check to see what is reflected in the mirror. I think this is the continuous condition of your zazen. This peeking to see what is in the mirror is what we call the function of the ego-self consciousness. This has to stop.

Another expression of Dogen's that is similar to "stepping backward to realize the Way" is "Setting up the self and carrying it forward to verify things is called delusion. When things come forth and confirm the Self, this is called enlightenment."

"Body and mind will drop away by themselves,
and the essential Self will be manifest. If you wish
to attain 'suchness,' practice 'suchness' immediately."

If you persevere in this practice of forgetting the small, individual self, body and mind will fall away naturally. "Suchness" means "thus," or "as-it-is." Don't wait until tomorrow to do the things I've been speaking about. Don't wait until you thoroughly understand the principle. Make the effort right now. "Immediately" means without the intervention of thoughts. There is an expression "to forget sitting." I would like you to absorb yourself in zazen to the extent that you forget sitting.

COMMENTARY 3
HOW TO SIT IN ZAZEN

The rest of the *Fukan-zazengi* is concerned with the actual details of where and how to sit. It deals with the best posture and the proper attitude to adopt when practicing zazen.

"For zazen, a quiet room is best. Eat and drink moderately."

The text so far has mostly been in the form of a preface. From now on, we come to the real core of zazen. In short, zazen is not a means. Since it already is the result, zazen is the condition where body and mind have fallen away. As zazen is already the end result, I would like you to understand that, in the case of Zen, it is not doing something from now on. Cause and effect are simultaneous. Please understand that zazen is not a means to attain something—it is the final result. The problem is that while we are already right in the middle of the result, we cannot verify it as our own. For that reason, even though we are the result itself, we search for another result. This is not in accord with the Dharma. Nevertheless, the habit of looking for results is brought about by the functioning of the ego-self consciousness. That is why it is necessary to forget this ego-self.

Why is it that we cannot directly verify the result as-it-is? I would like you to remember that this is due to "beginningless" ignorance. This ignorance is something that all past buddhas, including Shakyamuni Buddha and Bodhidharma, have certainly had. No one is born a buddha. I would like to emphasize this. Shakyamuni, before realizing oneness with the morning star, was in a condition of delusion and ignorance, just as we are now. His mind was not at peace, and he was in the midst of great conflict from which he could not be free. He was in exactly the same predicament as we are now.

It is best to practice zazen in as quiet a place as possible. Those who are new to zazen are particularly prone to distractions from outside. For this reason, choose a place with as few distractions as possible. Also eat and drink moderately—too much food will make us feel sleepy.

"Give up all deluding relationships and set everything aside."
From this point begins the explanation of the inner attitude for sitting. This is very important. "Give up all deluding relationships" means always to be one with objects, the things that are separate from us. When you are one with them, other things will never be a source of anxiety or concern. Objects are what you reflect: being one with what is heard, being one with what is thought. This means that you will not be turned around or shaken by circumstances.

If this point is misunderstood, then you will build a high wall between yourself and all other things. This would be a great mistake. Always be the object as-it-is, yet do not lose yourself. While you are one with all things, the Self is definitely present. This is what it is like when you give up all deluding relationships.

Willow branches are very soft and flexible. They bend with the wind. The following poem was written by someone watching a willow tree.

> Even in a wind it doesn't like,
> A willow tree is
> still a willow tree.

This is certainly not a condition where you have become an imbecile or are like a tree or a rock. It describes a condition where you are steadfast and yet also free to flow along with any wind or situation. I would like you to understand that the objective of Zen is, as aptly expressed by the willow tree's fluid nature, a truly soft, flexible mind.

"Do not think of good or bad, right or wrong.
Do not interfere with the workings of the mind,
nor try to control the movements of your thoughts.
Give up the idea of becoming a buddha."
This is the aspect of what we call "discrimination." Deluding passions, deluding thoughts, good and bad, right and wrong—let all things flow by as-they-are. "Do not interfere with the workings of the mind" means not meddling with your thoughts, which are the essential functioning of the mind. This is to entrust yourself to this function as-it-is, without bringing forth the ego-self. In other words, abandon and forget the ego-self.

Zen is the study of mind. If the mind is not disturbed, if it is peaceful, then there is no need for the practice of zazen. The mind is essentially always moving. This activity is the function of the mind. This means that it is a great mistake if a person tries by means of thought to stop the essential movement of the mind. There is no reason, though, to think that we can leave the mind to function as if it were a tree or a rock. The instruction we receive here is to let the mind function as-it-is, that it is necessary to let it move continually.

It is often said that if one is not sick, one does not need medicine. If you take medicine when you are not sick, it will, on the contrary, harm you. As I have already said many times, zazen is the final result. It is the condition where all things have been completely repented of. In this condition the ego-self has been totally extinguished, so there is no need to become freer. There is absolutely no need to worry about finding a way to forget the self.

"The workings of the mind" can be thought to refer to three different functions of the mind: care and attention, tiredness, and feeling pain. "The movements of your thoughts" signifies one thought arising, followed by other thoughts that pile up, one on top of the other. One of the Chinese characters we use for thought in Japanese is actually comprised of two components: the character for "object" on the top and the one for "mind" on the bottom.

"Zazen has nothing whatsoever to do with whether you are sitting upright or lying down."
As I said earlier, zazen is neither a way nor a means. Since it already is the end result, it is called the practice of a buddha. This means, then, that there is absolutely no need to get rid of distracting, deluding thoughts. There is no need to try to become a buddha. There is no need to try to be liberated. For that reason I would like you to understand that zazen is very different from what we usually think of as sitting upright or lying down.

"Usually a thick square mat is placed on the floor where you sit and a round cushion put on top of it. Sit either in the full- or half-lotus position. In the full-lotus position, first place your right foot on your left thigh and your left foot on your right thigh. In the half-lotus, you simply put your left foot on your right thigh."
Here begins the detailed instruction of how to sit. We sit on a round

cushion, which we call a *zafu*. This is used so that our legs do not begin to hurt. When sitting on the *zafu*, please sit with your back straight.

The half-lotus is half of the full-lotus position, so only the left leg is put up. But it isn't necessary to stick to this form. If your leg begins to hurt, it's fine to switch over and put the right foot on the left thigh. It is also all right to sit the way women often do in Japan, with their feet tucked under them. Or to use various kinds of seats or benches. In any case, don't worry too much about the outer form. I would simply like you to find a position so you can sit comfortably for a long time, without feeling too much pain in your legs.

In some of the bigger monasteries in Japan, if a monk could not sit zazen in the full-lotus position, he was not allowed to stay. In recent years, though, there has been a realization that this was an error, and slowly things have changed. I think this is good.

Why is it that only the outer form has become emphasized in this way? The reason is that the essential Dharma has been lost, and in order to at least pass down something, a lot of emphasis has come to be placed on form.

Apart from the *Fukan-zazengi* and the *Gakudo-yojinshu* (Points to Watch in Practicing the Way), Dogen wrote a piece called the *Fushuku-hampo* (Regulations for Eating in the Monastery), which explains in detail the way to eat. He also wrote the *Eihei-shingi* (Regulations for Monastic Life), which describes in detail the way to brush our teeth, rinse our mouth, wash our face, and even how to use a toilet. We hear of people who think that Buddhist practice involves faithfully following the rules that Dogen prescribed. This is a great misinterpretation. This is to practice in a very narrow, militaristic sort of way. There may be some people here who think that practice means strictly adhering to the form, with no deviation allowed whatsoever. They may like to do it this way and think it cannot be done in any other manner. I would like you to understand, however, that this is clearly taking place in a context where true zazen and the true Dharma have disappeared. For that reason, only the form is emphasized and rigidly followed.

If there are people here who are planning to build a Zen meditation hall and train Zen monks in the future, I think it would be a good idea for you to have the *Fukan-zazengi, Gakudo-yojinshu,* and *Eihei-shingi* on hand for reference. Those of you who have experienced group life are aware of the need for rules. Old-timers are familiar with the rules of the *zendo* so they can move and act freely without feeling bound by the rules. Without rules, group life becomes disordered. Please understand, then, that rules are a necessity in group life.

"Your clothing should be loose, but neat. Then place your right hand, palm up, on your leg and your left hand, palm up, on your right palm, with the tips of the thumbs lightly touching. Sit upright, leaning neither to the left nor to the right, neither forward nor backward. Be sure your ears are in line with your shoulders and your nose is in line with your navel."

Your belt or sash should not be tied too tightly. In the Soto Zen sect, the usual way to hold the hands is with the right hand underneath the left hand. In the Rinzai and other sects, there are some slightly different ways of holding the hands. Buddha statues often have the left hand underneath and the right hand above. In short, it is all right to interpret this to mean that we should hold the hands in a neat and orderly manner.

Sit with the backbone perfectly straight. Don't bend your back or let you head droop. Why is it necessary to go into the form in such detail? Ask Zen Master Dogen. When your nose and navel are in one straight line, you are not leaning in any direction.

*"Your tongue should be placed against the roof of your mouth,
with lips and teeth firmly closed. Your eyes should always
remain open."*

When you are sitting, keep your mouth closed. It isn't necessary to
keep your tongue in any special position; simply leave it in its natural place. If you keep your eyes open, you might need to blink more,
and it is also easier to be distracted. It is best to leave your eyes half-
open, neither open too wide nor shut.

There is one point you must be careful of. Some practitioners want
to concentrate their energy so it flows from the top of their head to
the area of the hips. These days the word "energy" is often used, and
some people think they must put energy in a particular place. But if
you direct energy in a certain way, it means that consciousness is ac-
companying the sitting form. This means that the direction of your
zazen is very different from that indicated by Dogen. He said that the
true form of zazen is "formless."

Dogen repeatedly gave detailed instructions on sitting upright with
the back straight and the head upright, without directing energy to
any particular place. This way it is possible to breathe most naturally
and comfortably.

*"Breathe gently through your nose. Having adjusted your
posture, take a deep breath. Sway your body to the left
and right, then settle into a steady, immobile position,
sitting like a mountain."*

Breathing through the nose is the quietest way to breathe. It is important to breathe softly. If you make a noise like a bellows when you
breathe, you will disturb those around you. "Take a deep breath" includes both a long inhalation and a long exhalation. If you take two
or three deep breaths, you can expel negative energy, but you must
do it quietly so people next to you cannot hear you. When we begin

to sit in zazen we should inhale deeply and exhale slowly. If you have been sitting for some time and your mind becomes disordered or agitated, at such times, too, please regulate your breath while breathing deeply.

Some people plop themselves down on their *zafu*, but it is important to sit down quietly. Once you are seated, rock your body slowly to the left and the right in order to adjust your sitting posture. As you begin zazen, first sway with a large movement that gradually becomes smaller. These movements are reversed when it is time to get up after sitting.

Sit like a mountain that is disturbed by nothing. In other words, sit being empty. Dogen said, "The seal of Buddha Mind is imprinted on the three activities." The three aspects of zazen—actions, speech, and thoughts—are given physical form in the full-lotus position. They are the example and model of a buddha. Zazen of the body is to sit solidly, without moving. This is "sitting like a mountain." As there is nothing to say while you are sitting, you rest the tongue against the roof of your mouth. This is zazen of the mouth. Zazen of the mind is to give up the idea of becoming a buddha. It is not thinking good or bad, right or wrong. This is zazen of the mind, the third aspect. Both from the aspect of posture and mind, zazen itself is Buddha.

"Think of not thinking. How is this done?
By leaving thinking as-it-is. This is the essential art of zazen."
These are the words of the Thirty-sixth Ancestor, Yakusan (known in Chinese as Yaoshan). They are a direct quote from an answer he gave to a monk's question, and the words apply to our practice of zazen. "Leaving thinking as-it-is" refers to a condition where the ego-self has disappeared, a condition where no "impurities" are mixed in. You may not be able to understand directly a condition where there is no self, but observing and perceiving essentially takes place without

a "me" who is supposedly doing these things. It is simply the function of observing and perceiving as-it-is, without the ego-self.

"Think" may easily be interpreted to mean that we must think something, but actually it refers to the function of No-Self as-it-is. Regardless of whether it is something with form or not, please understand this to be "thinking as-it-is." The condition of "thinking as-it-is" is beyond thinking and not thinking. In short, it is the condition where there is no room for the ego-self to enter. "Not thinking" and "non-thinking" are often used in English translations of the *Fukan-zazengi*, but if you try too hard to understand them, it will create confusion. "Not" and "non-" can be understood to be synonymous with liberation from the ego-self.

I think there are many of you who think, "I must not think," so you suppress thought. This is the worst thing to do. You are suppressing the natural flow of the Dharma itself. Don't think of trying to suppress thought. By thinking, "Don't think, don't think," your essential nature is lost. Without any freedom or comfort, you only end up sitting and thinking of trying to get rid of suffering. This is the sickness of not knowing that the thought of getting rid of suffering is suffering.

In order to have you understand this really well, I will say it one more time. Zen is neither thinking nor not thinking. "When there is thinking, there is only thinking, and while thinking, there is liberation." And "when not thinking, there is only not thinking, and while not thinking, there is liberation."

Zazen is not something to be learned from a teacher. Zazen is something learned by means of zazen itself. This is why we say "zazen is zazen." I would like you to verify this yourselves through "real practice and real inquiry."

Although this may seem far removed from our zazen right now, please absorb yourself in your zazen practice. That is "thinking as-it-is." Again and again I ask you to make an effort to be wholeheartedly in a samadhi of zazen.

All things are transient. All things are without self. All things are in the peace and tranquillity of Nirvana. These are the "Three Seals of the Dharma": impermanence, no self-nature, and the freedom of Nirvana. Even if your mind is agitated, it won't be that way forever. So I would like you, with peace of mind, to flow with reality right now. This is the main point of zazen.

"The zazen I speak of is not 'step-by-step, learning Zen.'"
Furthermore, a consistent attitude is necessary in practice, which is described in this part of the *Fukan-zazengi*. "The zazen I speak of" is the true Dharma transmitted from Shakyamuni Buddha. This is the zazen of Dogen, which is very different from that of other people. "Step-by-step, learning Zen" stands in opposition to "beyond learning." Both "learning Zen" and "beyond learning" are expressions used in Zen, but the difference between them is like that between heaven and earth.

"Learning Zen" is to use Zen as a means, or a way, to seek some result in the future. It creates a division by perceiving zazen as something outside, and then utilizing it to learn something gradually. In contrast to this is "beyond learning." This affirms the result, which is directly and completely finalized as-it-is. This is "suchness," or the thing itself as-it-is. This is the big difference. It is in this sense that Dogen says, "The zazen I speak of is not 'step-by-step, learning Zen.'"

Bodhidharma, the Twenty-eighth Ancestor after Shakyamuni Buddha, went from India to transmit Zen in China, which is why he is also called the First Ancestor of Chinese Zen. At that time the teaching of Buddhism in the form of sutras had already reached China, but there was no Zen. At the temple of Shorin-ji (Shaolin-si), Bodhidharma always sat quietly facing a wall. Seeing this, scholars of the time said he was "a man of learning Zen."'" It was even written in books that he was obviously a practitioner of "learning Zen," and references were made to him as the "learning Zen Brahmin." This was very mistaken.

Why did Dogen say that zazen is not "step-by-step, learning Zen"? At that time in the Tendai and Shingon sects, Zen similar to "learning Zen" was widely practiced. These days some people confuse zazen with meditation, but they are completely different things. Zazen—the Zen correctly transmitted by buddhas and enlightened ones—has no source or base. There is absolutely no standpoint, foundation, or standard. That is zazen. It isn't something from which a standpoint has been created in order to learn something else. "The zazen I speak of is not 'step-by-step, learning Zen'" especially emphasizes that people will be confused if "beyond learning Zen," which has been properly transmitted, and "learning Zen" are mixed together, like jewels and pebbles. These days, though, gravel is confused with jewels. Unfortunately, since people don't have the eye to tell the two apart, the present situation is that people do not know what is true and what is false.

In a Japanese monastery, the evening meal is called *yakuseki,* and a dish we often eat at this meal is called *zosui.* This is a mixture of rice, leftover soup, and assorted vegetables, served like a soft porridge. Mistaken Zen is a one-pot mixture of "learning Zen" with yoga, various things similar to Zen, and true Zen. We call this "zosui Zen." It fills the stomach. For the person eating it, whether it is "learning Zen" or some other form of Zen, it is easy to think it doesn't matter so long as the stomach is full. Be very careful about this point.

To repeat myself again, there is no foundation to the Zen and zazen that has been correctly transmitted by buddhas and enlightened ones who have transmitted the Dharma. There is no source or origin. There is absolutely no standard. However, for "learning Zen" and other practices that resemble zazen, there is always a source. There is a standard. The thing that is the source and that makes the standard is "me"; it is the ego-self. It becomes a very different kind of zazen if the ego-self is the basis for it.

"It is simply the Dharma gate of comfort and ease.
It is the culmination of totally realized enlightenment."
The zazen of the correctly transmitted Buddhadharma is the result itself. As the form or shape of zazen right now is the result, it clearly transcends even cause and result, the law of causality. Comfort and ease is the condition where the body is comfortable and the mind is at peace. This means that zazen is the clear manifestation in an instant of all the 84,000 Dharma teachings that Shakyamuni expounded during his lifetime. Zazen, or "the Dharma gate of comfort and ease," is the expression of all the Dharma teachings in one reality.

Zazen is enlightenment. It is the condition in which the supreme Way has been completely brought to an end. There is nothing remaining, either before or after. It is the condition where in each instant everything is truly and totally realized. That is why we say "practice and enlightenment are not two." Yet many people in the Soto Zen sect misunderstand this and end by making a great mistake. This is the sickness of perceiving the teaching and then using it. In other words, many people think that shikantaza is the "culmination of totally realized enlightenment," and for that reason there is no need to seek anything more. They say there is no need for enlightenment, and so everything is all right as-it-is. They stand up to teach others making the grave error of saying, "Everything is all right as-it-is. Simply sit zazen, that is enough." This is mistaken, and if there are any people here sitting in this manner, I must ask you to stop immediately.

Excuse my repeating myself, but I must emphasize that from the standpoint of the Dharma it is certainly true that there is nothing to seek and no enlightenment to be attained. But from the point of view of *you as a person*, this simply isn't so. This means that it isn't good to get stuck in a place where you use the Dharma by perceiving it. I want you to understand in this regard that Zen is the study of the Self.

"It is the manifestation of ultimate reality.
Traps and snares can never interfere with it."
The original meaning of *"koan"* was a law established by the country. As it was law, it was something that people could not violate. "Ultimate reality" refers to the condition right now as-it-is. "The manifestation of ultimate reality" (which Dogen referred to as the *genjo-koan*), then, is things as-they-are. Things themselves are totally free in any situation. They cannot be caught by "traps and snares."

Understand that your everyday life is "the manifestation of ultimate reality." Forgetting yourself in each thing, each instant, each moment—this is what we call zazen.

Before Kanchi Sosan became a monk, he went to see Taiso Eka, the Second Ancestor of Chinese Zen and Bodhidharma's successor, to ask about the Dharma. Sosan was afflicted with leprosy, which at that time was believed to be a sickness brought about by bad karma. Sosan went to Taiso Eka and said, "Please make repentance for me and release me from my bad karma." Eka replied, "Well, then, bring your bad karma here." After some time, Sosan said, "I thought I could find my karma, but I can't find it anywhere." Eka said, "In that case, you are released from all karma, aren't you?" At that instant Kanchi Sosan became greatly enlightened and was cured of his illness.

A "trap or snare" is a condition in which you are bound by something you cannot see, like karma, for example. If you enter by the door of zazen, it is easy to fall into the trap of thinking that zazen is only sitting. For that reason I would very much like you to understand Zen within movement so you can make an effort to be each thing, each activity, each moment.

Regarding karma, I would like to touch briefly on the problem of good and evil. In Buddhism, evil is said to be those things that interfere with or hinder the practice of Buddhism. The source of these evils or hindrances is attachment to the ego-self. Essentially there is no self. To think there is a self when in fact there isn't is ignorance. To perceive the self, then, is evil. It is a complete hindrance to the practice of the Way. It is the same with karma. The ego-self is perceived to exist out of ignorance. Karma is the functioning of the ego-self and all its activities, which take place within that ignorance. This is the cause of transmigration through the realms of delusion.

Please be aware that both good and bad karma are created by the perception of the ego-self. For that reason, both good karma and bad karma must be eliminated. However, the true nature of all of these things is that they are without form. True nature means the essence of things. The essence is formless, which means there is no shape or form. For this reason all hindrances caused by evil deeds return to emptiness. This is the Buddhist viewpoint with regard to karma as well as good and evil.

"If you attain this, you are like a dragon that has reached
water or a tiger that reclines on a mountain.
The true Dharma then appears of itself, and you will be free
of dullness and distraction."
We can make the significance of zazen our own within our everyday life by means of the success of Zen in movement and Zen in stillness. Then we will be like "a dragon that has reached water or a tiger that reclines on a mountain." This is a condition of great majesty. There will be a complete change. This is the effect of zazen.

"Dullness" refers to a state in which a person knows much about and is attached to a conceptual understanding of emptiness. In such a condition, it is not possible to function in a world that is full of different things. Everything has become equal or the same and there is no freedom. There are some people who can do nothing when their mind becomes quiet. In fact, this kind of stillness is a condition unconsciously created by the ego-self. This stillness is easily mistaken for the condition where there is no good or bad, no hot or cold, no up or down, no east or west, a condition where there is absolutely nothing. If a mistake is made about such a condition and it is left like that, it will turn into a great sickness—a Zen illness. Please be very careful about this point.

In contrast to this is "distraction," the opposite of equality or oneness. It is a condition of being too much engaged in difference or discrimination. In such a condition, the mind is scattered, unfocused, and restless. There is no calmness or peace. There is no power to change because you are stuck in the world of difference.

If you work at Zen within movement and Zen within stillness in your everyday life, then these deluding passions of dullness and distraction will naturally disappear. If that happens, "the true Dharma then appears of itself." The true Dharma is the Dharma itself, zazen itself. In other words, if you endeavor to be zazen itself, there will be absolutely no room for dullness or confusion to enter. This is "the direct transmission from mind to mind," the true Dharma Zen transmitted by Bodhidharma.

This is the reason Dogen made a great distinction between "learning Zen" and "beyond learning." The form or sitting posture of learning Zen and zazen of the true Dharma is exactly the same. It is impossible to differentiate between them by simply looking. At this point I must say, as I always do, that Zen that waits for enlightenment isn't good. It is completely mistaken to think that by working at zazen, delusion and the passions of greed, anger, and ignorance will gradually disappear and a quiet condition where "body and mind are cast off" will be attained. Please understand that this attitude should not be adopted.

PART II
BEING THOROUGHLY FAMILIAR WITH THE TRUE SELF

IN THE WHOLE UNIVERSE, THERE IS ONLY YOU

In what way can you become familiar or intimate with your true self? Zen, the Dharma, and the Way point the direction. Consequently, Zen, zazen, and the Way are all means to take us to the world of the Dharma. Many people, though, are greatly mistaken on this point. They think it is sufficient simply to do zazen, or simply to seek the Way, and this is the end of it for them. I would like to explain why this type of thinking is mistaken.

The present population of the earth is said to be almost six billion, or even more. This means that each of us is one of these six billion people. Each of us is irreplaceable; we each have our individual existence. This is something that must be clearly discerned. First, we must see our own essential Self, and then it is necessary to make sure that we live our lives with our feet firmly on the ground. We are each one part of six billion people, and we must ascertain that we are truly the only person in the whole universe, someone who doesn't need to rely on Buddha, the Dharma, or the Sangha. This is the first step in being familiar or intimate with the true Self.

YOU ARE BOTH ZEN AND THE WAY

I would like to tell you a story from China. You may be familiar with the name of Joshu, who was a priest long ago. One day a monk asked him, "I am just a beginner in the practice of Zen. Please teach me how to do zazen." Joshu said, "Have you eaten breakfast?" "Yes," replied the monk, "I've had plenty for breakfast." Joshu said, "That's fine. Then wash your bowl and put it away." At that point the monk, who had resolved to seek the Dharma was just beginning the practice of zazen, said "I understand. Now I realize the direction of practice." So he went off happily.

There is an important point in the story for those of us who practice. We tend to think of our eating bowls as things that are outside of us. Yet Joshu said, "Wash your bowl and put it away." What does the bowl signify? You yourself. Each one of you must clean yourself thoroughly and then bring the matter of the ego-self to a conclusion. If Joshu's words are not understood in this way, a great mistake will arise.

We perceive Zen, the Dharma, and the Way to be outside of ourselves. But it is a serious error to create a distance between yourself and these things in this manner. If you make a separation between yourself and what you are looking for, no matter how much effort you make to lessen that distance, that effort will be in vain.

It is a mistake to look for something that is far off in the distance. The Dharma is something that is everywhere at any time.

▊ YOUR REALITY IS ZEN

I come from Japan, but Zen, the Dharma, and the Way do not exist solely in Japan. Zen, the Dharma, and the Way—these are things that cannot be exported. Since they cannot be exported, they cannot be imported. Consequently, that which has been imported from India, China, or Korea in *not* Zen, the Dharma, or the Way; these are each of you—your reality *as-it-is*. The reason I say this is so that you will understand that reality *as-it-is* is Zen, the Dharma, and the Way.

But if you do not "walk the Way," it will never be possible to reach your destination. The first human being to awaken and realize he himself was the Way was Shakyamuni Buddha. It was not the case, however, that he grasped something new. For those who believe in the Way of the Buddha and aspire to practice Zen, it is only natural that they will practice in the manner taught by Shakyamuni Buddha and the enlightened ones of India, China, and Japan who transmitted the Dharma.

If you clearly and certainly walk the Way, you will awaken to yourself. However, if you create a distance between yourself and Zen, the Dharma, and the Way, even if you walk the Way, I think you'll always feel great anxiety as to whether you will be able to truly realize the Way or not.

Since the Way and Zen is your condition as-it-is, there will definitely come a time when you realize, "Ah! So that's how it is!" There is no doubt about this. It will take longer for some of you to reach this point than others, but nevertheless you will definitely realize it. For some people it has taken thirty years to realize themselves, it took Shakyamuni six years. Others have realized in a single day. It varies from person to person. However, it will undoubtedly happen.

Shakyamuni Buddha gave the following example to indicate how certain this is: If you hold a stick in your hand and aim for the ground below you, no matter which way you strike the ground, it is impossible to miss it. In the same way, it is impossible not to come to an understanding of the true Self if you seek the Dharma and Zen.

DO NOT FORGET YOUR TRUE SELF

There is a story about a priest named Zuigan. Each morning, on awakening, he would always address himself, saying, "Master, master!" which could also be translated as "True Self, true Self!" He would ask himself, "Master, are you awake?" He would answer, "Yes, yes." And then he would say, "Don't be fooled by others." Whereupon he would answer, "No, no." This was his practice.

We are apt to forget our true Self. "To forget" means that we are always out traveling and away from home and so our home—or body—is vacant. We will be in a condition where we always think that sometime in the future, eventually, we must return home.

You may be familiar with the great thirteenth-century Zen master, Master Dogen. At first he traveled to China in search of the Way. This was a condition in which his true Self was absent. But then he met Tendo Nyojo, another Zen master, and was able to "cast off body and mind." How did he express what he had attained?

> The eyes are horizontal
> The nose is vertical.
> I won't be fooled by others.
> The Buddhadharma does not exist in the least.

In another story, old Master Joshu said, "Before I knew that the Way is myself, I was used by time. But after I realized that the Way is myself, I was no longer used by time. Now I am able to live using time." For Joshu, hot was still hot, cold was still cold, and pain was still pain. He was still the same person—and yet depending on whether Joshu realized his true nature or not, he lived being used by things or he lived being able to use things.

The fact is that each of you possesses the same power as Joshu. By becoming intimate with Zen, you will understand how it is possible to find and master this power. When you do, each of you will be Joshu, Dogen, and Shakyamuni Buddha.

THREE PRINCIPAL TEACHINGS

In Buddhism there are three principal teachings: all things are impermanent; all things are without self-nature; and all things dwell in the peace and quiet of Nirvana. The first of these—all things are impermanent—means that there is no condition that is fixed or deter-mined for any length of time. It is not a matter of there being one thing that is undergoing change. It means that things—including yourself—are always changing and are without a center or an essence. As human beings we are always perceiving through the senses, which means that we are cognizant or aware of things. We can only perceive past and fu-ture. All anxieties—the opposite of peace of mind—as well as agita-tion, restlessness, and haste, arise from either the past or the future.

As I said earlier, the present moment is a condition where there is absolutely no separation between yourself and things. This is not to say, though, that there exists such a thing as the present moment. The condition we refer to as "now" is one where there is truly no gap between yourself and other things. When you don't have peace of mind, this means that you are in a condition in which you are con-stantly aware of a distance between yourself and other things. In our present life, regardless of whether we know it or not, we are one with things. This is what is meant by the challenging expression "all things are impermanent."

No one remembers the time when they were born, the time they emerged from their mother's womb. In the same way, there is no one who knows their own death, thinking "I've just died." We know nei-ther our birth nor our death. We first become aware of ourselves at the age of three or four. If we live to the age of eighty, during the in-tervening years we experience many things that are good and bad. There is gain and loss, there is this thing and that, but whose life is it? This world of perception and cognition—what we usually think of as the way human life must be or should be—this is all the life of the ego. Zen is the means that can help you discover the true nature of the ego.

When people are asked to give proof that they are living, they often cite the fact that they can see and hear and feel things. But this is not proof that you are living. It is merely a description of living. You perceive your self, the ego, "me," and then simply describe your present condition by saying that because you can see and hear and feel you are living. Someone who is dead cannot, obviously, describe what the condition of death is like. The reason is that it is already their reality. There is a problem of how to demonstrate the reality of living without description.

Even if you are aware of minute changes within the flux of events, you must understand that it is the ego that knows it and not the true Self. This means that with regard to our whole life, as long as the thing we call "me" does not stop intervening, it is not possible to lead a life that is truly free and peaceful. You already are free, but since you want freedom, you lose it. Consequently, it is necessary to free yourself from thinking that things must be this way or that way. This too is the meaning of the first teaching, "all things are impermanent."

The second teaching states "All things are without self-nature." As all things are selfless, this means there is no possibility of grasping on to something as your unchanging essence. For example, imagine it is now 8:00 in the evening. Let us say we go to bed at 10:00 and drift off to sleep without knowing it. While sleeping, who knows that they are asleep? Most likely, there is no one who is aware that they are fast asleep. In the same way, when we awake, it is not possible to be aware of awakening. All you can do is, by perceiving "this thing" (the body), say you are "awakened." But who is it, through perceiving "this thing," that calls it "you"?

No one can think two thoughts at the same time. If you were asked to think a good thought and a bad thought at the same time, it would not be possible. Have you ever considered why it is not possible to think two things simultaneously? Whether you think about this or not, you are yourself and you are living your own life. In fact, it is not possible to think of yourself. This means that it is not good to insert your own egoistic opinions. If the ego-self intervenes, it means that inevitably you will see things by comparing them. Zen practice is the practice of letting go of that intervention of the ego-self.

The third teaching is that "all things dwell in the peace and quiet of Nirvana." As I said at the beginning, Nirvana, or true peace of mind, is something that we must not seek elsewhere. As long as you seek it elsewhere, you will never be free of feelings of satisfaction or anxiety. If we open our eyes, even when seeing something for the first time, we can clearly see all of it. If you hear something for the first time, you can hear it perfectly. You are endowed with the free functioning of the senses. This means that no matter what you see or hear, you assimilate all of it. You have the power to digest things in this way.

In a life where there is no separation, there is neither peace of mind nor anxiety. When there is peace of mind, there is also anxiety. In a world of the true Dharma, there is neither peace of mind nor anxiety. Having said that, there may be some people who wonder, "Then why is it necessary to practice?" But really try living "now." There is no room for thoughts like peace of mind and anxiety to enter in. In this way, no matter how insignificant or important something may be, whether for yourself or for someone else, forgetting yourself and immersing yourself wholeheartedly in your work and making an effort, that is the life of Zen. It is the life of the Way.

People often speak of doing something for this or that purpose but in Zen we do not live our lives for this or that purpose. Even if we are doing something for ourselves or for someone else, the life of Zen is to forget all that comes before and after and really do each deed for the purpose of the deed itself. Wholeheartedly applying yourself to the task at hand, exhausting yourself in each activity, that is the life of Zen. Consequently, I would like you not to understand Zen, the Buddhadharma, or the Way by means of your intellect or your education.

Although I have just said that all of our life is Zen, the Dharma, and the Way, actually these things do not exist.

NOTHING IS BETTER THAN SOMETHING GOOD

In everyday life, we often hear people say, "Now I can really believe it." But as long as you are satisfied with "really believing," it means that there is still belief. You must forget belief. It is the same with fact and reality. If you think something is true or real, it means you perceive "real" or "true," and there remains a gap between you and "real" or "true." The life of someone who has realized the true Dharma is one where there is *no* reality. In other words, it is to dwell peacefully in the world *now*.

There is a Chinese proverb that says: "Better than something good is nothing." Zazen is a wonderful thing. But even though it's wonderful, *nothing* is better. The reason is that something good is a condition on the way to the ultimate. We do not know if it will become better or worse. The key to zazen is to "grind up" zazen by means of the practice of zazen. If you follow through with this, then no matter what you are doing or where, each activity can be called Zen. When zazen is finally completely ground up and disappears, then for the first time everything is truly the Way, Zen, the Dharma. This is what is called "everyday mind."

Finally, I would like you not to simply understand Zen or the Buddhadharma conceptually. It is fine to investigate what others have said or written in books. But to say, "I've understood something that I didn't understand before," that is not Zen practice.

NANSEN CUTS THE CAT

Consider this koan from the *Book of Serenity (Shoyoroku)*, "Nansen Cuts the Cat":

> There were about 500 monks training under Nansen. The monks slept in one hall that was divided into east and west. One day the monks were fighting over a cat. Seeing this, Nansen picked up the cat and said, "If you can say anything, I won't cut it in two." No one spoke, so Nansen cut it.
>
> Later, Nansen told Joshu what had happened. Joshu immediately took off his sandals, put them on his head, and walked out. Nansen said, "If you had been there, you would have saved the cat."

This particular koan originated in China 1,200 years ago but it is not just a story. I would now like to explain why.

Nansen is the abbreviated name of Nansen Fugan, a famous priest of Tang China. Nansen cut a cat in two, and this cat is the central problem of this koan. Three people or groups of people appear: the monks who are asked the question, Nansen, and Joshu—plus the cat. Each of you are now Nansen, you are now the monks being asked the question, you are now Joshu, and you are now the cat.

An argument began among some of the monks concerning the cat. "Does the cat have buddha-nature or not?" "In the future, will it become a buddha?" "Can it do zazen?" They argued about the Dharma and Zen just as we do every day. While the monks were arguing, Nansen appeared and picked up the cat by the scruff of the neck. He said to the monks, "If you can say something about this cat, you will save it. If you can't say anything, I'll cut the cat in two."

In your heart you wonder, "What is Zen? What is the Way?" You have been practicing zazen for a long time, but will you really be able to attain the wonderful results related by the buddhas and enlightened ones? These were the questions the cat represented. If you become the cat, then you will clearly understand. Or if you become the monks, I think you will also understand. Nansen, by picking up the cat by the neck, symbolically demonstrates to each of us the need to get a grip on the questioning mind. "How will you resolve this?" You must understand Nansen's question this way. It is as if Nansen appears in front of you and asks, "How will you deal with this matter?" For those of you who have this questioning, inquiring mind, this questioning mind is the cat. For those of you who practice *shikantaza*, this *shikantaza* is the cat.

In this koan, you must be able to give the answer immediately, "Say it now." Understand this is your problem. "Out with it!" Can you clearly awaken to your essential self? That is the meaning of this case. None of the monks could answer Nansen—how would you answer? Have you been able to get a firm grip on the cat or not? Perhaps, while you are sitting zazen, the inquiring mind is clear, and perhaps you understand clearly how to practice shikantaza. But when you are eating or doing work, doesn't the cat get away?

The Way as well as Zen must be everywhere at any time. If Zen or Zen practice exists only when you think of it, then you will never be able to resolve the problem of the cat. Whatever we see or hear or feel, everything we experience is buddha-nature. In the case I have related, it is written that Nansen cut the cat in two. But is it possible to cut buddha-nature in two? Please consider this. If you are "just" sitting, you will get stuck in "just." The reason I am presenting this case is so that you can check and see to what extent you are "just" sitting. How do you see the cat? I am waiting to hear your answer.

None of the monks could answer Nansen, so he finally cut the cat in two. Joshu was out working when Nansen cut the cat, but when he returned, Nansen said to him, "Today a problem arose concerning a cat, but none of the monks could give an answer, so I cut the cat in two. How would you have answered?" On hearing this, Joshu put the sandals he was wearing on his head and went outside without saying anything. Whereupon Nansen said, "If you had been there, it would have not been necessary to cut the cat." The problem this koan represents for us, then, is how we will answer so that the cat is not cut. I would like you to be Nansen, the monks who were asked the question, Joshu, and the cat. While you are in this condition, thoroughly think through this case.

All of the buddhas and enlightened ones who appear in collections of Zen sayings and records are you. They are speaking about each one of us. This story comes to us across twelve centuries, but if each of you save the cat, then Nansen as well as Joshu will be resurrected.

THE DELUDING PASSIONS ARE ENLIGHTENMENT

Within our minds, there is a cat called "greed." There is also a cat named "anger" and another cat called "folly" or "ignorance." In Buddhism, we call these the three deluding passions. These passions or desires are the source of all our suffering. However, if there was no greed, we would not be able to do zazen. Without anger, the determination and enthusiasm not to lose out or be beaten would not arise. Without ignorance, there would be no reflection or introspection. For these reasons, I would like you to understand that greed, anger, and ignorance are also other names for buddha-nature. It is only because we are used by greed, anger, and ignorance that we have come to think of them as being bad.

Shakyamuni Buddha also said that the deluding passions are themselves enlightenment.

If you sit in shikantaza and let whatever thoughts appear and take no notice of them and do not deal with them, then they will definitely turn into enlightenment. You may recall the expression "everyday mind is the Way." Anger, ignorance, greed, as well as all kinds of anxiety, impatience, and irritation, exist within the "everyday mind." This is called "everyday mind *as-it-is* is the Way." I would like you to realize that it is a mistake, then, to throw away something bad that is inside us. In Buddhism, however, everything is buddha-nature, so there is nothing to throw away. The problem lies within your thoughts, or how you think. Inevitably you cannot accept your thoughts, so you create a distance between you and them. But, as I often say, zazen is the way to verify that you and your thoughts are one. We practice so we can confirm this.

THROWING YOURSELF INTO ZAZEN

I will digress for a moment to speak of a man named Toyohiro Akiyama. He is a reporter working for TBS, a Japanese television company. Some time ago, he was sent into space on a Soviet rocket. Later, when he returned to Earth, he was asked, "While you were in space, did you have any kind of religious experience? Have you returned with any philosophical impressions?" Akiyama replied, "I was already so preoccupied with my affairs here on Earth that I experienced absolutely nothing different on venturing into space."

As I always say, as long as you do not truly bring a resolution to the ego-self, no matter how wonderful a universe you travel to or whichever world of God or Buddha you may reach, there will be no change. Throw yourselves into zazen and really forget your own thoughts. With this kind of practice, you will certainly be able to meet your true Self. Please believe until belief is no longer necessary.

HYAKUJO'S WILD FOX

Consider this koan:

> Whenever Master Hyakujo gave a *teisho*, or Dharma talk, an
> old man always came to join the monks and listen to the
> teaching. When the monks left, the old man would also
> leave. One day the old man stayed behind. Hyakujo asked
> him, "Who are you who stands before me now?" The old
> man said, "I am not a human being. In the days of the Kash-
> yapa Buddha, I used to live on this mountain. One day a
> monk asked me, 'Is an enlightened person also subject to
> causality or not?' I said 'No, he is not.' Since then I have lived
> the life of a wild fox for five hundred lifetimes. I now beg you
> to say a few words on my behalf to release me from my life
> as a fox. For that reason I ask you, 'Is an enlightened person
> also subject to causality or not?'" Hyakujo said, "Such a per-
> son is not blind to causality." No sooner had the old man
> heard these words than he became greatly enlightened.

If you could not quite become completely one with Nansen's cat,
perhaps you can become one with Hyakujo's fox. This case concerns
cause and effect and appears in every collection of Zen koans. It is regarded as very difficult. The particular problem dealt with is whether
a person who is enlightened and "finished" with practice is subject
to the principle of cause and effect or not.

First of all, let me speak about the principle of cause and effect. It
is said that if you wish to know a past cause, then look at the present effect, the present result. There is always a continuum of past,
present, past, present. We cannot say that the past is only something
that happened long, long ago—it also is five minutes ago, or even a

single moment. Your condition now is inevitably attributable to past causes. The present circumstance also becomes the cause of some future outcome.

With regard to breathing, each breath is new. So too with thoughts. When one idea or thought arises, that is birth. When one idea or thought vanishes, that is death. Always there is a constant repetition of birth and death. This repetition continues through past, present, and future.

We are in the habit of perceiving "this thing" (this body) as "me." The reason for this is that from birth we have come to believe that things exist. In fact, though, they do not—but we usually cannot accept this. This is the meaning of "all things have no self-nature." If there is a center, essence, or permanent self-nature that is perceived, this is a delusion. Similarly we make errors about time; we can only perceive time either through the past, which has already gone, or by the future, which has not yet come.

Consider the method of zazen in which we practice counting breaths. If you reach "two," for example, then "two" is everything. There is no "one" or "three." "Two" is all. At that point, you should have truly forgotten yourself and cast off body and mind.

Nonetheless, we perceive that something that does not exist does exist. This is the ego, which inevitably becomes the center of what we perceive. For this reason we are in the habit of seeing things and comparing them in terms of good and bad. Consequently, it is easy for people to think that if all bad things could be eliminated, only good things would remain. Nevertheless, good and bad exist only in contrast to each other. If all bad things were to disappear, then it stands to reason that there would no longer be any good things. If one half of a duality were not to exist, its opposite would also not exist. Please understand this clearly as we explore the principle that cause and effect are one.

In the teaching of Buddhism, everything is taught from the standpoint of the *result*. This means that for those people who have not yet reached the final result, it is not possible for them to say that they either understand or do not understand simply by looking at the teachings of Shakyamuni Buddha or of the enlightened ones who have transmitted the Dharma.

The *"dharma"* of *Buddhadharma* means a natural principle or law. Every aspect of our life is the Dharma. There is the Dharma of bad and the Dharma of good. There is also the Dharma of understanding and the Dharma of misunderstanding. Moreoever, these two are not in opposition. Our condition now is one that is already separate from good and bad, enlightenment and delusion. We are always peacefully dwelling in a condition where there is only the result itself. Yet, in order to awaken to the condition, it is necessary, by means of Zen, to let go of our dualistic viewpoint of comparing good and bad.

Results unavoidably correspond with causes. There should be no feelings of surprise or disappointment. If our efforts result in failure, it is only reasonable to be content with that result. The same applies to successful results. If there is a successful outcome, the requirements for this success were present, so there is nothing to be happy about. Similarly, do not feel disappointed in failure. Nevertheless, people can be seen to be selfish because when we have some success, we are naturally pleased with that success, and when we encounter some failure, by comparison we are not happy.

Returning to the case about Priest Hyakujo: Why then, on answering "does not fall under the principle of cause and effect" did the priest become a fox? And why on hearing "not blind to cause and effect" did the old man again become a human being and realize great enlightenment? What is the degree of difference between "not falling under cause and effect" and "not being blind to cause and effect"? Investigate this problem; generate this inquiring mind.

The point of this case is whether the wild fox is at peace with being a wild fox. If the fox could truly be one with being a fox, then it would not want to become human. To be a fox would be enough. The state of being truly satisfied as a fox is what we call being "a buddha." On the other hand, a human being who is not satisfied with being human and who constantly looking for something else is seeking to be a buddha; this state we call being "a wild fox." This is a very difficult problem.

In Buddhism, we speak of transmigration though the six realms. These realms are the six worlds of delusion: heaven, human beings, hell, hungry ghosts, animals, and fighting devils *(asuras)*. As long as we are deluded, we can never live peacefully as human beings. If you cannot be at ease with your present situation, you will forever be seeking something else. This is a condition where you will go around and around, migrating through the six realms, never feeling settled. Essentially, though, regardless of whether we are a being in hell, a human being, or a being in heaven, we must be able to exist peacefully in these respective worlds.

In Zen, we have the expression "unblemished" or "undefiled." The Japanese word for this, *fuzenna*, literally means "not-dyed-dirty" in other words, "untainted." Many people understand this to mean that if you practice and achieve a certain strength or power through that practice, no matter which world you go to, you will not be dyed the color of, or be sullied by, that world. But this is a great mistake. "Unblemished" or "undefiled" means to be *completely* dyed that color. If you go into the color red, then you are completely dyed red. If you enter something white, then you completely become the color white.

In the Rinzai Zen sect, the expression "be master of yourself wherever you are" is often used. If this expression is misunderstood, it will be misunderstood in the same way as "unblemished." If you cannot be truly at one with the world you live in, you will always see other worlds as being beautiful and wonderful. The words "not falling under the principle of cause and effect" and "not being blind to cause and effect" are concerned with this condition of not being settled, of not accepting your situation.

The main purpose of practice is to bring an end to the seeking mind and to live accepting your present circumstances. It is important that you sit in zazen and are content with the result. As you sit, inevitably the thought arises that somehow or other you should be able to sit better. This is a fact. But sit without thinking that because you cannot sit well, you want somehow to sit better. If you cannot sit well, then accept it and leave it that way. If you are not settled, then accept it and leave it that way. I would like you to make the effort to live peacefully in whatever condition you are in.

To be truly what you are without being jealous of someone else is what we call Buddha. However, if a person cannot peacefully accept being a person, he or she will always want to be a buddha, to experience enlightenment. We liken this condition of trying to seek peace of mind to that of a fox. Think this through carefully as you continue with your practice.

In Japan, a fox is regarded as an animal that tricks people. Please practice steadfastly and confidently without being tricked or misled. If a fox is tricked by a fox and continues being tricked, that is all right, but it isn't good to set up the ego-self with the attitude that you cannot be tricked.

THE DAILY PRACTICE OF ZEN

Zazen can broadly be divided in two: Zen within activity and Zen within stillness. Zen within activity embraces the other activities in our life, such as our work and so forth. Zen within stillness is what we do in the *zendo*, the meditation hall.

I would like to speak practically about how you can continue with Zen outside of the meditation hall, outside of retreat. Everyday life itself is Zen. As I have already said many times, drinking coffee, eating toast, washing your face, taking a bath, these are all Zen even though we do not label them Zen. I would like you to be clear about this. Consequently, there is absolutely no need to choose between activities that are Zen and those that are not. Believe this firmly and have unshakable confidence in it. Then let go of this faith. This is the way I would like you to act, but in practice this is not easy. It is a mistake for you to incorporate into your life things you have learned about Zen through books or by listening to others. This also includes the Zen practice you have done up until now.

There is an expression in Zen "to put another head on top of the one you already have." This is a mistake. It really is not possible, and I want you to take great care not to make this mistake. Even though I say this, I am sure you will live and experience many things, learning by trial and error. You make an effort to build up your practice, but then you become lax and it falls apart. Again you make an effort to build up your practice, but again you become lax and it falls apart. It is important not to give up. While living your everyday life, I ask you once again not to adopt or bring Zen into that life. Apart from those times when you are sitting quietly, I would like you to forget completely about Zen.

I also have some comments about formal sitting, Zen within stillness. Make sure to sit each day. Thirty minutes is fine, fifteen minutes is fine. The length of time will depend on your circumstances, and these vary from person to person. Be sure to set aside some time to sit every day. At that time, no matter how much you are concerned about your work or what is happening in your household, forget those things and sit in a *samadhi* of zazen.

From the beginning, I would like you to divide your life into Zen within stillness and Zen within activity. In this way, I believe you will be able to be one with your work and be one with a *samadhi* of zazen. If you do this, I believe you will not even have time to think "this is Zen." Then, during Zen in stillness, you will be able to forget yourself and be one with a *samadhi* of zazen.

Continue to persevere: building up your practice, it falls apart; again building up your practice, it falls apart. In this way, I am sure there will come a time when it is no longer necessary to divide Zen in two.

CONTINUING WITH PERSEVERANCE

It is not easy to sit zazen. Zen practice is a difficult thing. Please do not lose heart and give up along the way. It is not something that must be concluded within a set number of years. Nor is it something that, if not taken care of quickly, will prevent you doing something else. I would like you to persevere steadfastly. That is what we call "continual mindfulness."

There are three things that any person who aspires to the Way of Zen must do: asking a master about the Dharma, the practice of zazen, and observing the precepts. Many people ask me how they can know if the zazen they are practicing is correct or mistaken. I will give you some guidance about this.

Mistaken zazen and mistaken guidance result when, figuratively speaking, the teacher first makes a suit of clothes and a pair of shoes into which you must make yourself fit. This is a grave error. A similar mistake occurs when the teaching prescribes that you mimic the teacher's form until the teacher releases you from the form.

In Zen it is said that all the teachings of Buddhism and Zen are "skillful means." They are like a finger pointing at the moon. If you look in the direction indicated by the fingertip you will see the moon.

The object of the teaching is to see the moon. However, the moon and the finger are one. If you are taught that the moon and the finger are separate, this is mistaken. In simple terms, as long as you do not understand, skillful means exist as skillful means. However, when you come to understand Zen, you understand that the means are also the result itself.

If you truly attain the Way, you will no longer have to think about yourself. Since it is not necessary to think of your own matters, it is possible to concentrate one hundred percent on your work, on the needs of others, and on your own families. In this way, you will feel great ease and comfort. This is the practice of a bodhisattva, the activity you are doing now becomes the practice of the bodhisattva. Please continue your endeavors diligently.

SITTING IN ZAZEN

While you are sitting, keep your back straight, leave your eyes open, look down over the bridge of your nose, and quietly regulate your breathing. Please practice zazen this way until a signal is given. How can sitting quietly be in accord with the Way of Buddha? I would like to speak in concrete terms about how it is possible to transcend life and death by means of sitting.

We are not conscious of our breathing. I don't think there is anyone here who is consciously exhaling, inhaling, exhaling and inhaling. However, in Zen practice, you are asked to be aware of your breathing. This is something that is unavoidable, even though it would be better not to have to do such an inconvenient thing as to be conscious of breathing. So: concentrate on your breathing: inhaling, exhaling, inhaling, exhaling—one breath at a time, gently, carefully, sincerely. I would like you to repeat this again and again—inhaling, exhaling, inhaling, exhaling. By watching the breath—in other words, by concentrating on it—I think you can gradually enter a samadhi of breathing, a samadhi of awareness.

However, as long as you are conscious of samadhi, it means that the "you" who is conscious of it is still outside the samadhi. If you are truly in samadhi, it is not possible to be conscious or perceive that you are in samadhi. The condition of being conscious of the breath and of trying to enter samadhi is naturally something that you are aware of. To be aware of this is not a bad thing. What I would like you to do is to "grind up" consciousness by means of that awareness— grind it up like sesame seeds in a mortar. It may take some time to enter samadhi or to "grind up" consciousness by means of consciousness, but if you persevere in being conscious of the breath, it is certainly possible to enter *samadhi*. When you watch the breath single-mindedly and enter samadhi, you forget that you are conscious of the breath. To forget in this way means that you will return to the condition when you were unaware of your breathing.

In the beginning, this may seem troublesome and complicated. Nevertheless, Zen practice is the process of first knowing something and then, by means of "grinding up" that awareness, returning full circle to the beginning. Looking at someone's outward appearance, it is not possible to know if that person is aware of his or her breathing or not. And yet, if two people are in the same state or condition and are leading the same kind of life, one person can, while being conscious of his or her breathing, walk the Way. It is certainly possible for such a person to attain liberation. In contrast, the other person is doing nothing except simply sitting. For this person, there is no liberation. Consequently, there is the difference of heaven and earth between them.

■ PUTTING AN END TO
THE DISCRIMINATING MIND

The zazen in which by watching the breath you forget you are breathing is something you cannot see with the eye or know directly. So let me explain what it means to truly see something.

Consider a vase of flowers. On seeing these flowers—in the first instant you perceive them—you probably did not think "beautiful" or "these flowers suit me" or "these are such and such kinds of flowers." You simply saw them. This is what we call "right seeing," the most correct way of seeing. But then thoughts arose, such as "they're beautiful" or "I don't like these flowers." This second perception arises incredibly quickly. Such conscious perceptions as "beautiful" and "ugly" have no relation to the thing seen. As they have absolutely no relation to the flower itself, discriminations such as "like/dislike" or "beautiful/ugly" only arise from within your own mind. As long as we continue to make such discriminations with our minds, it will not be possible to see the flower as it is.

Human beings have six sense functions: seeing, hearing, smelling, tasting, touching, and thinking. Although these functions are all different, we are never confused by them. They are mysterious functions. No matter how complicated a thing may be, at once we can see it, hear it, think it. It is impossible to see it mistakenly or to hear a sound mistakenly. Moreover, there is no guiding center inside that gives us orders such as "see this" or " hear this" or "feel this." This means that the condition of allowing these six functions to be as they are is the most peaceful condition for human beings.

There is a method of zazen called "*shikantaza*," which means "to sit single-mindedly." *Shikantaza* is to sit entrusting yourself to thoughts as they arise. It is to sit in a dignified matter, without being moved by what is seen, heard, or thought; shikantaza is to sit without being bothered in any way by these things. By continuing to entrust yourself in this way to the six sense functions as they are, it is possible to know that you are one with things. This is what we call "casting off body and mind."

In China, Dogen practiced with Zen Master Nyojo, and he cast off body and mind doing this kind of zazen. He went to Nyojo and said, "I have cast off body and mind." Nyojo said, "No. It must be 'body and mind cast off.'" The reason why "cast off body and mind" is not correct is that from the beginning, body and mind have already been cast off. Consequently, Nyojo explained that casting off body and mind is wholly unnecessary.

"DONE, DONE, FINALLY IT IS DONE!"

Shakyamuni Buddha sat single-mindedly for six years. Then, at dawn one day, he saw the morning star and had great enlightenment. Yet he had no one to instruct him how to sit watching the breath or letting the senses function as they do. He sat wholeheartedly, but he still could not really understand. For that reason he was completely exhausted both in mind and body. He was so tired he was like a worn-out rag.

Looking at the morning star, he was one with it. This was such a strange and mysterious thing that he uttered the *gatha,* or verse, that we recite at the end of the Heart Sutra *(Hannya Shingyo).* You are probably familiar with the verse: *Gaté gaté parasamgaté bodhi svaha.*

Gaté gaté means essentially "I've done it!" or "It is completed" or even "Finally, it has been accomplished." He yelled this word twice, *gaté gaté,* on seeing the morning star and finally was able to cross an impassable mountain. *Gaté gaté parasamgaté:* "without a doubt, certainly it has been done."

Parasamgaté conveys "I thought it was only my suffering, but I have been able to cross over together with all sentient beings." *Bodhi svaha* is a cry of joy—"Hurray!" "Rejoice!" "It is finished." "Enlightenment has been accomplished." "Finally, I have crossed over to the other side." In various Buddhist countries, there are many interpretations of this last line of the Heart Sutra, but I think this way of reading it conveys the essence.

The matter that we must direct our attention to is that Shakyamuni said he was able to cross over *together with all sentient beings*. He crossed over with all of us. To awaken to satori and see the true nature of the Self, what we call *"kensho,"* is not something that happens for only one person. This awakening takes place together with all sentient beings. If it is not like that, then is it impossible for it to be a true awakening, or satori. This is expressed in the Buddhist teaching that all things return to one, that all things return to the Self, and that the Self is all things.

The *satori*, or awakening, of Shakyamuni was not merely an experience that took place 2,500 years or so ago. It is the condition of each one of us now. In the same way as Shakyamuni Buddha, each of us can be awakened at any time—as Buddha was when he saw the morning star, or in the way Kyogen was brought to enlightenment when he heard the sound of a rock hitting a piece of bamboo. All of us are endowed throughout the day with the opportunity to realize liberation through casting off body and mind.

With regard to the way of sitting that I mentioned earlier, it is an extremely troublesome and complicated matter. However, without it, even if you were to encounter the condition of seeing a star, hearing a rock strike a piece of bamboo, or any other circumstance or opportunity that might bring about awakening, you will pass them all by. It is not useful simply to sit in a vague, dull sort of way, even if it makes you feel good and you are quiet and at peace.

BEING ONE WITH
THE QUESTIONING MIND

I would like to speak about Gensha, a monk who practiced under Seppo and the means by which he attained enlightenment. Gensha had been with Seppo a very long time. Thinking that he would not be able to complete his training—in other words, that he would not be able to know the true Self—he decided to change masters. He left the monastery at night. As it was still dark as he was descending the mountain, he happened to stub his toe on a rock, tearing off his toenail. Gensha gave a yell in pain. At that moment, he thought, "I've been taught that there is no self. But now, on losing my toenail, suddenly there is incredible pain. If there is no self, then where does the pain come from?"

I think it often happens that when people are instructed in zazen they are told not to think, that it isn't good to think. But it's not like that. By means of thinking "where does the pain come from?" Gensha was able to forget himself. If you can live your life always at one with the questioning mind (what we call "genjo-koan"), then by coming in contact with the appropriate circumstances this questioning mind will completely disappear.

Changing masters was no longer a consideration for Gensha, so he returned to Seppo. He told Seppo what had happened and that it was no longer necessary for him to go elsewhere. Finally, Seppo certified his realization. In this way, regardless of whether we practice zazen or not, if we live at one with the questioning mind, or of we live leaving everything as it is, without interfering with it, it is possible to clarify the true Self through meeting the condition that will bring about liberation. Age, gender, religion, and length of experience practicing zazen make absolutely no difference. I would like you to think a bit about the focus of your life, the goal that you have set your sights on. Do not make the excuse that you do not have time to practice zazen or that since you believe in another religion it isn't possible to listen to what I say. I would like you to try to incorporate zazen into your life.

THE WAY IS ONE

Zen Master Dogen wrote, "You should know that what is important is not a matter of debating whether a teaching is superior or inferior, or of assessing the depth or shallowness of a teaching; all we have to know is whether the practice is genuine or not."

There are many kinds of religion, each with its own teaching. We should not debate and discuss which is better or which is worse. Nor should we talk about one's personal understanding—"this person really understands, that person's understanding is still shallow." It is not a matter of saying, "I used to practice like this," or "formerly I had such and such an experience." The question is how you are sitting now, right now. The question is how you are living right now. In what way do you see and hear things? The most important thing is to be here now, the *now* of now. This means living just hearing the sound of the insects and all the other sounds that can be heard. It is a way of hearing. Or being one with the questioning mind.

This is what is important. This is the teaching that asks us if our condition now is one where enlightenment can really be attained or not. In other words, is our condition now one that enables us to put an end to the ego-self or not?

There are many, many different religions, each with their own believers. I have no wish to deny their authenticity or denigrate them. If people, regardless of their religious beliefs, can incorporate the method of practice I have explained here, all ways become one. Then each person can truly become free and peaceful through his or her respective religious beliefs. Don't think, then, that it is necessary to renounce your religion and change to Zen because the Zen teaching is superior. I would like you to honor your religious beliefs as they are, and while doing so incorporate the mind and teaching of Zen into your everyday life. This is the way to a complete and fulfilling life.

PART III
AWAKENING TO THE TRUE SELF

WHAT IS SESSHIN?

I would like to say a few things concerning sesshin, our retreats of intensive meditation practice. In our everyday life, with all its troubles and complications, we often lose sight of our selves. Accordingly, when those who aspire to sit quietly and practice zazen in order to awaken to the true Self come together for a certain period of time, we call this *sesshin*.

The Japanese word *sesshin* is written with Chinese characters that can be interpreted with two meanings. They can mean either "to focus or unify the mind" or "to put the mind in order." Not only zazen but many forms of spiritual discipline and practice have a similar aim. However, one aspect concerning focusing, unifying, or putting the mind in order makes the content and direction of the practice of zazen very different from other similar disciplines or practices. This point is embodied in the question, "Where in the vast universe is the mind to be put in order?" "This thing," which we call the body, is not separate from other people, from the universe, mountains, rivers, trees, or grass. There is no division. The big problem, then, is by what standard can we measure whether the mind is in order? If some means or method is used to order or unify the mind, it implies that there is a clear distinction between something that is in order and something that is not in order. If, for example, zazen is used as a means to order or unify the mind, there are necessarily two things: the part that is in order and the part that is not. No matter how long you continue, there will never come a time when you can say, "Yes, it's finished. The mind is unified and in order."

When I speak of ordering or unifying the mind, this is not something done gradually as a process by quietly practicing zazen. The fact is that all things are already in order, and beyond that there is no need to do anything. The aim of sesshin, then, is to realize that this condition—where everything is already unified and in order—is our condition right now.

Any person can think clearly about either the past or the future, but very few people have truly realized the present, the moment right now. "Present" or "right now" can also be expressed by such terms as *nyoze* (suchness, or as-it-is-ness), *ku* (emptiness), *mu* (nothingness), "*do*" (the Way), or "Zen." Or if we look for an even broader meaning, it could be called "*ho*" (the Dharma, the Truth, or the Law).

The Dharma exists everywhere. It exists everywhere, regardless of place, culture, creed, language, or race. Therefore, as I talk to you now, it isn't a matter of having you understand or listen to my Dharma. The Dharma is not something that belongs to any one person. It belongs to anyone who attains it. It is unbiased and unblemished; it is something unborn and imperishable. It is the condition of each of you right now. All things, including yourself, *are* the Dharma. Since each of you is the Dharma itself, there is the possibility that here, right now, without resorting to any ways or means, you yourself can directly verify this. *Sesshin* is concentrated practice in experiencing your own Dharma by yourself.

Nevertheless, a beautiful flower does not always bear fruit. The fruit is the most important thing. So my strong hope is that as a result of a *sesshin* you can make the flower bloom and become a wonderful fruit.

Zazen isn't something that takes place only in the zendo. I would like you to remember that every activity, whether we are working, eating, or walking, must be sesshin. Working, eating, washing our face, sleeping—every activity is merely a changed form of zazen.

▨ KYOGEN'S QUESTIONING MIND

Long ago in China there lived a man named Kyogen, who was extremely intelligent and erudite and had an excellent memory. He trained with his master, Isan, and was so clever that he was able to comprehend ten times as much as he was taught. However, because of his cleverness he couldn't awaken to the true Self while he was with Isan. Kyogen made a great effort to forget his ego-self, yet he continually thought, "In this lifetime with this body, I'll never be able to realize what Isan is telling me." For that reason he decided to leave the monastery, and he went to live in a hut in the quiet of the mountains. There he completely gave up on practice and training.

In this case, to "give up," or "let go," or "put down" doesn't merely mean to throw away or forget your ideas about Zen or your understanding about practice. It is a condition where "this thing"—the body/mind itself—is thrown away. Why, then, did Kyogen still not understand the Truth? The reason was that the thought of having thrown away the ego-self still remained. Kyogen still could not realize the condition of "body/mind completely cast off" or that "essentially it has always been thrown away." He was discontent for this reason, and that is why he went to live in the mountains.

Isan, in his teisho, had always said, "Things as they are are all right. Simply to accept without resistance that which is seen, heard, or tasted is enough." But Kyogen could not accept it that way. This was his "questioning mind." Taking this questioning mind, Kyogen went to live in the mountains in order to become questioning mind itself.

One day while Kyogen was sweeping, a pebble moved by his broom hit a piece of bamboo. It was at that moment that his questioning mind became one with the sound of the pebble hitting the bamboo. He became one with that condition. He then completely understood what Isan had always been talking about.

I think you have often heard and read expressions such as "awakening to the true Self" or "realizing satori." But this doesn't mean that there was an "I" who awakened or an "I" that became realized. The meaning is that "this thing" became the condition or circumstance itself. To become one with conditions in this way is the most important point of Buddhist practice.

WHAT IS "THIS THING"?

"This thing," which you all think is yourself, is neither you nor anyone else. It is nothing whatsoever. It is one and the same with everything. Therefore, "this thing" is the most suitable expression to describe it. The functions of seeing, hearing, smelling, tasting, touching, and thinking are functions of "this thing" and belong neither to you nor to anyone else. Our lives are constituted by the coming together of the tool-like functions of the six senses.

"This thing" is comprised—if we specifically divide it in this way—of the physical body and the mind. The physical body is the shape or form. It consists of the four elements: earth, water, fire, and air. All things are made of these four basic elements. The Heart Sutra teaches that form, sensation, perception, formation, and consciousness—the five *skandhas*—are completely empty. Of the five *skandhas*, form or matter is the condition in which things are seen, the condition in which "this thing" sees. Sensation, perception, formation, and consciousness are mental functions and cannot be seen. The six sense functions (including thinking) enter through the medium of the physical body. The mental functions in turn arise upon the stimulation of the body's six sense functions. I think you can see that the physical body and the mental functions do not work separately.

Of the mental functions, consciousness is the one we must be most careful of. All things are said to possess buddha-nature, but consciousness, perception, or cognition are things only human beings have. Buddhist practice and training is based on a person clearly understanding this matter of consciousness. Because this is so important, I would like to elaborate on it.

The important point I would like you to grasp is that the moment you perceive or think of "this thing," then "this thing" or "you" exists. In the Agama Sutra we find the following words: "Because *this* thing exists, *that* thing exists. If *this* thing doesn't exist, *that* thing doesn't exist." This explanation is consistent with the concept of emptiness that we find in the Heart Sutra that we chant each morning, or with Buddha's teaching about wisdom. As it says, by perceiving the ego-self, all things come into existence.

That these things come into existence is not a problem in itself. It becomes a problem because we make it one. This is to say that before what is called "I" comes into existence, all things in the universe are already there. With the coming into existence of the ego-self, the things of the universe are perceived as objects. This perception leads to the labeling of such things as "nature." Mountains, rivers, trees, and grass—these things of themselves are neither nature nor not nature. People have merely labeled them as such. In the same way humans have recognized and labeled all things, and by so doing have brought about the separation between people and other things. While it often seems as if these things that have been labeled by you are the cause of your confusion, in fact it is just the opposite. To think that the cause of the problem is anywhere other than yourself is a big mistake. It is complete delusion. This is the proof of the statement that by investigating and examining yourself, all anxiety can be completely eliminated. There is no doubt about this.

▨ "EVERYDAY MIND IS THE WAY"

Joshu asked his master, Nansen, "What is the Way?" The "Way" here refers to the "Way of Buddha."

Nansen replied, "Everyday mind is the Way." "Everyday mind" is our daily life. In other words, it is every activity in our ordinary life from the time we rise in the morning until the time we go to bed at night. But when "everyday mind" is expressly pointed out in this way, you immediately reflect on the condition of your life and say, "So that's what it is. My condition right now is 'everyday mind.' It is the Way of Buddha." Immediately you perceive your condition in this way.

Before you began to practice zazen or heard the words "everyday mind" though, there is no reason to believe that you were aware of the concept "everyday mind." To be unaware of it has no connection with understanding or not understanding. Rather, you can say that you were always living a life of "everyday mind." You were always within the Way and never apart from it.

On hearing the words "everyday mind is the Way," a perception arises, and this perception creates a gap, a division. The division of "Ah! So this is the Way!" is created. At that point, because Joshu couldn't understand "everyday mind," he asked again, "If 'everyday mind' is the Way of Buddha, then how can I know it? What kind of practice should I do in order to understand 'everyday mind'?"

Reading this, you may sense something special the instant you see the expression "everyday mind." Similarly, when you hear the word "Way," you have the feeling that there is some special Way that exists. Thus, when you perceive a word, whether it is heard or read, you immediately attach a meaning to it. In Zen, you should not attach a special significance to "everyday mind" or to "the Way."

Joshu was later to become a great Zen master, but at that time,

because he did not understand at all, he attached a special significance to "everyday mind" and "the Way." It seemed to be getting
even more confusing, and that is why he asked, "What kind of practice would be best?" Nansen gave him a surprising answer: "If you
seek for it, you'll only go in the wrong direction." If you begin something that seems like practice with the intention of trying to understand "everyday mind," you will only separate yourself from it all the
more. If you are thinking of practicing in order to look for the Way,
you will only get farther and farther away from it. It is as if, while
walking the Way and being right in the middle of it, you start looking around for it, wondering where it is.

Yet Joshu still could not understand. So he asked the following
question: "As I don't understand now, if I never begin to practice,
won't I *always* not understand? Without practice how will I ever understand the Way?" If a person doesn't seek for the Way, doesn't try
to understand, and doesn't practice, wouldn't the Way always remain
not understood? Without resorting to some means, wouldn't a person
always not understand the Way? Nansen said, "The Way is neither
knowing nor not knowing. Knowing is illusion, not knowing is
indifference." The Way is neither something to know nor something
not to know.

If you think you know what the Way is, then it is delusion. If you
don't know what the Way is, it is indifference. It is apathy. To see
clearly what is right in front of you was Nansen's answer. To penetrate this koan please become Joshu.

The main point of this dialogue is: "Knowing is illusion, not knowing is indifference." As I said earlier, the six sense functions are all
separate from what you think of as yourself. All that exists is the
thing as-it-is. Whether we know it or not, there is only the function
itself as-it-is. It isn't possible to attach any significance or value by
means of human thought, or to cling to anything by believing or not

believing. Our condition is always just as-it-is without the least trace of a cloud. It is completely clean and bright. If even a small doubt arises, it is never caused by something outside of us. The ego-self in opposition to itself has created it. It does seem strange, then, that while we can clearly be aware of our confusion, we don't know what to do about it.

To have just seen something, to have just heard something, means that the event has already passed. The perception that something was seen or heard remains only in your thoughts. The ego-self does not exist but is "perceived" to exist. In this way delusion is created.

"The Way is neither knowing nor not knowing. Knowing is illusion, not knowing is indifference." This is a concise explanation of this reality. This dialogue wasn't merely an exchange of words. Nansen's true intention was to have Joshu understand the condition in which it is impossible to perceive the ego-self. That is why he used the expression "knowing and not knowing."

Our zazen practice is essentially a matter of awakening to the true Self. This true Self cannot be perceived. It is vast and without limit. To awaken to this true Self is also expressed as awakening to "No-Self," or "No-Mind," or "Emptiness," or "to forget the ego-self."

All things, including people, are never fixed in the same condition from moment to moment. In the midst of this constant change, there is no central thing, nothing we can perceive as the ego-self. The teaching of Buddhism is the matter of awakening to the fact that originally there is no self. "No-Self" means to awaken to a self that is so vast and limitless that it cannot be seen. Something that can be seen has a limit—it is small.

Zen practice is the most direct way to awaken to the true Self.

And yet it will not do to "know" Zen; when that happens you have a Zen style of life and you do Zen practice. It is regrettable to use Zen in this way; it is a mistake. There is no need always to hold on to what you have learned. It is necessary to forget both what you have learned and what you know now. It is at that point that you begin to lose the distinction between doing zazen and not doing it, between the time you are practicing and when you aren't practicing. This doesn't only apply to Zen. Believing or not believing, liking or disliking, understanding or not understanding—there is no need to hold on to these things. When we say "everyday mind," this is something that is neither in the past nor in the future. It is the very thing itself and cannot even be said to be the present. The expression "neither knowing nor not knowing" signifies the condition where the thing itself cannot be perceived. This is also your present condition. It is what you are always doing in the moment "now."

After having heard about "everyday mind," I think you may go out to work and do various other things viewing your actions in terms of "everyday mind." But I would like you to forget all about it, throw it away, let go of it. If you continue your practice in this way, I am sure that, without fail, you will truly encounter the boundless Self. Again and again, I would like to remind you that once something is perceived, the actual fact is already gone. Please don't go chasing after things as you perceive them.

ACCEPTING YOUR CONDITION NOW

The purpose of zazen is to find great satisfaction in every moment, down to the smallest detail of your everyday life.

Simply to be able to abide peacefully in the law of cause and effect can be said to be the end result of zazen. To serenely accept and live with your condition right now as the result of cause and effect means that the need for any kind of apology or excuse on your part disappears. Most people live their lives constantly apologizing or making excuses for the state in which they find themselves. This is because the ego-self is perceived to exist in opposition to the law of cause and effect. Not to make excuses means, for example, that if you feel anxious you don't seek for peace of mind. By becoming anxiety itself, as-it-is, all things are resolved. If we had to find satisfaction in opposition to a condition of dissatisfaction, we couldn't say that it is as-it-is. Satisfaction created in this way will disappear over a period of time. That satisfaction will give rise to the next dissatisfaction.

At this point I would like to touch on the subject of believing and not believing, a matter that often creates confusion. I am not referring to the simple faith or belief in Buddha or God by which people come to complacently accept their dissatisfaction, or by which people rationalize their condition in terms of cause and effect. This type of believing and not believing is of no use to us in our Zen life and practice.

Things that we can see and hear do not exist because we believe they do. And regardless of whether we believe in things or not, satisfaction does exist. It exists apart from a person's thought. That which exists separately from the thought of the ego-self and with which there is no room for interference on the part of the ego-self is called "the Dharma."

Belief and non-belief are also like this. If something is truly believed in, the object of belief disappears. True belief must go so far that the object of that belief must be discarded, must be released. This also applies to liberation. If something has truly been liberated, then actually there is no object that has been liberated. Neither should there be a distinction between those who are liberated and those who are not, nor between before and after liberation.

In essence, the Buddhist teaching, the object of Zen practice, is that you liberate yourself. It isn't as if we come to Buddha with blind faith and are saved by some efficacious means. Zazen is the practice of liberating yourself. It is nothing other than awakening to the true Self.

Since you don't know the true Self, for some reason or other you find something lacking in a part of your daily life. There is some dissatisfaction. When life is the life of the true Self, all dissatisfaction, anxiety, confusion, and irritation disappear.

ARE YOU AWAKE?

The teaching of Buddha *is always* the conclusion, the sought-for objective. In order that people don't mistakenly go in the wrong direction, the objectives or conclusions are clearly indicated from the beginning. There is a Japanese Zen expression *"Hogejaku."* This expression is often interpreted as "to throw away or give up everything," implying from now on. But this isn't what it means. Rather, the meaning is that "everything has already fallen away or been thrown away," and it points to your condition right now.

Another expression is *"Seiseijaku"* The meaning of this phrase is "Are your eyes open? Are you really awake?" It is a question to ask yourself, to which you reply, "Yes, yes." Again it is not a matter of awakening at some time in the future. Instead, you accept that your eyes are already open, that you are already awake. It means that in any situation there isn't something you must do from now on. Whatever you do and whatever you think, everything is already finished.

You may be able to accept that all things are all right as they are. However, it is extremely difficult to accept that you yourself are all right as you are with regard to the Dharma. For that reason it becomes necessary to practice zazen, and by so doing make an effort to reach the Dharma. Those who want to attain true freedom or peace of mind, those who want to awaken to the true Self, those people practicing zazen are also the Dharma. The thing being searched for is also the Dharma, which is to say that the Dharma is looking for the Dharma. The idea of satori, or liberation, seems strange if both the thing looking and the thing being looked for are the Dharma. But the fact is that if you do not grasp the Dharma and if you don't truly become the condition where there is "no thing," there will always remain some aspect with which you cannot agree or are not satisfied.

Shakyamuni Buddha said, "With this stick I hold, I hit the ground." There was absolutely no way he could miss hitting the ground. In the same way, if you practice zazen you will surely be able to attain freedom, peace of mind, and satisfaction. This is absolutely certain. If those of you who are seeking the Dharma truly believe this, and endeavor to practice zazen with this certainty, then you will surely attain this liberation.

SHAKYAMUNI BUDDHA'S PRACTICE

Some 2,500 years have passed since Shakyamuni Buddha died. He was the first human being who, through his own efforts, found a way to save himself. The four sufferings of birth, old age, sickness, and death confront modern people in exactly the same way as they did Shakyamuni so many years ago. The pain of birth, the loneliness of old age, the anxieties caused by sickness, and the fear of death—Shakyamuni wondered if it might not be possible to be liberated from these four sufferings. It was for that reason that he left his father's palace and started to practice.

These four sufferings are the reason for the basic pain and confusion in our lives, and all other sufferings can be traced back to them. In addition, four more sufferings may be added to make eight. These are:

1. *The suffering that comes from separation from those we love.* This is the suffering that comes from the inevitability that while we are in the world, we will surely be separated from those we love and who are important to us. The biggest suffering and

sadness for us, though, is caused by death, which stands in opposition to the ego-self that we love so much.

2. *The suffering that comes from being together with those we hate.* This is the suffering that comes from the inevitability that we will have to live together with people we dislike or hate, when, in fact, we would rather not; we might even go so far as to wish to harm and kill them. This is the suffering of extreme hate.

3. *The suffering that comes from the fact that we cannot have what we want.* This is the suffering that arises because we can never find exactly what we desire, or all that we desire, no matter how hard we look.

4. *The suffering that comes from the fact that the physical body is a vessel of suffering.* This is the suffering that comes from our attachment to the five *skandhas* that form our body, mind, and environment. This means that "this thing" is like a vessel in which many kinds of suffering are collected. As long as "this thing" exists, the above-mentioned sufferings will continue to accumulate.

THE DELUDING ATTACHMENT TO THE EGO-SELF

Before Buddha's enlightenment—before he awakened to the true Self, before he forgot the ego-self—no one knew that the ego-self did not exist. In order to liberate himself from suffering, he thought it would be necessary to undergo some kind of physically demanding ascetic discipline. He therefore spent three years of study and ascetic training with the greatest philosophers and teachers of his time. He trained so severely during those three years that no one before or after him surpassed his effort.

However, he became aware that there was something mistaken in the direction of this kind of practice. He realized that if his body were to disappear, at that point all other things would also disappear. If this happened, there could not be some eternal, unchanging Truth. If something comes to an end, it is not the real thing.

Shakyamuni realized that there must be a way to free people from the suffering of their everyday lives. He also saw that ascetic practice that often verges on death is not the way to find this liberation. He realized that even if he reached some level of understanding through ascetic practice, it would be a useless endeavor if it only lasted while he was alive.

The birth of "this thing" is something that we do not remember. Consequently, the fact that you are dead is also something you cannot know. "This thing," which knows neither its own birth nor death, is what is now living. Understanding things, seeing, and hearing—exactly what is it that is understood, seen, or heard? Since it is all created through consciousness, it is nothing other than the ego-self. Through attachment to this ego-self, we create all kinds of anxiety, pain, and confusion. This is the attachment of the ego-self to delusion. To completely free yourself from this attachment by yourself, by your own efforts—to make this an actuality—this is Zen practice.

ALL THINGS EXIST WITHIN THE SIX SENSE FUNCTIONS

Everything in the world, and even something as vast as the universe, exists within our six sense functions. It is absolutely impossible for something to exist somewhere other than those sense functions. If the ego-self is forgotten, the separation between yourself and a certain condition or circumstance vanishes, and all things become empty. At the same time all other things in the world are also forgotten. This includes all things of the past, present, and future. In the same way, these things become empty.

Many people have a misconception concerning enlightenment. They think of it in terms of a certain experience at a particular moment, but the real essence of enlightenment is beyond compare. If there is a "before" and an "after" the experience of enlightenment, it is not the real thing. It is impossible to know the Way of Buddha or the true Self as long as there is any intervention of the ego-self, no matter how much effort is made.

WHAT IS THE TEACHING OF THE BUDDHADHARMA?

The teaching of Shakyamuni Buddha is one of selflessness, of no ego-self. But this wasn't a teaching born out of the thought of a man named Shakyamuni. What is referred to as the Dharma is something that was *pointed out* by Buddha. The teaching of Shakyamuni Buddha is the Dharma itself. The Dharma completely fills the universe. It exists everywhere. However, because no one tells you that things of themselves are the Dharma, our condition is one in which, while living right in the middle of the Dharma, we aren't aware of it. Also, since there is a lack of teachers who can expound the true Dharma, people often end up searching in vain only to find the fossilized skeleton of the Dharma. Practice can also merely become a way or a means to grasp this fossilized Dharma.

The Twenty-eighth Ancestor after Shakyamuni Buddha was Bodai Daruma (as he is known in Japanese); he is more commonly known as Bodhidharma. He was the first to bring Zen from India to China, although the first Buddhist sutras had already appeared in China some four hundred years before. The teachings of Buddha in the form of written sutras can be said to be like a finger pointing toward the moon. Although there was much enthusiastic study of these sutras, the essential point, "What is the Dharma?" was still not realized. With Bodhidharma's arrival in China, however, he personally verified that he himself was the moon.

We can be sure that there were many differences in the culture and customs of India and China, but the Dharma transcended all those differences. It is all-embracing and beyond comparison. After the Dharma had been transmitted to China by Bodhidharma, Zen began to thrive and was passed down from generation to generation. Even at that time China was a big country. Nevertheless, Bodhidharma was the only person in all of China who could expound the true Dharma. Subsequently, through the efforts of Dogen, who went to China and transmitted the Dharma of Bodhidharma to Japan, it is possible for those of us here today to practice zazen.

IN JAPAN ONLY THE FORM OF THE DHARMA REMAINS

The situation in present-day Japan is that, unfortunately, only the external form of the Dharma remains, only a shell. The finger is pointing at the moon, while the moon itself is disappearing. The Soto Zen sect has fallen into a kind of Zen that says superficially "Just sitting is enough," or "It's all right to sit just as you are." People are taught that in "just sitting" there is nothing to seek and nothing to throw away. But in this way they perceive "just sitting" and don't realize that this idea of "just" must also be thrown away in order to truly be one with reality as-it-is. The Rinzai Zen sect, on the other hand, has fallen into one of the pitfalls of koan Zen, whereby Zen is thought to be a matter of looking at different koans in the manner of progressively climbing up a series of steps. In both these sects, masters have all but disappeared who can guide us with the teaching that we must awaken to the true Self and that we must forget the ego-self, in other words, that we must become liberated.

This is an extremely sad state of affairs. In the middle of this chaotic world, the way of liberation for all people is revealed by the Way of Buddha. Whether you are a lay person or a monastic, please seek the Dharma, please become someone who actualizes this way of liberation. If this Way were to disappear, all people would lose sight of the direction of Zen practice. It is now thirty-five years or so since I began zazen. What is important is not the length of time I have been doing it but rather that I was able to meet a true teacher, and for that reason I am now able to speak to you in this manner.

As far as the Dharma is concerned, all that is necessary is that you concentrate on the reality of the moment right now. That is enough. Thoughts arise like "my legs hurt," "I don't know what he's talking about," "I hope this talk will end soon," or "Now I really understand." Aren't these and all your other thoughts the actual fact of your reality right now? All you have to do is, without resisting, simply accept this reality right now, your reality-as-it-is. If you could really concentrate on this reality and become one with it, I think you could then freely expound the Dharma, the way of liberation, in the everyday words of your native language. This would be a wonderful thing, since freedom and peace of mind could then be imparted to many people.

SELF-TAUGHT ZEN VS. ZEN THAT IS IN ACCORDANCE WITH THE DHARMA

In Japan, many arts are associated with the Way, such as the way of tea, or the way of flowers, or the way of archery. Among these different arts is calligraphy, the way of writing. The basis for calligraphy is the stroke for the dot. Japanese characters are all merely variations on the shape of this basic stroke. According to the way a person executes the dot when applying the brush, it is easy to see at a glance if he or she is studying with a qualified teacher.

The question, then, is whether the way a dot is drawn in its various forms matches or agrees with the conventional way of using the brush. If we have practiced zazen for a long time but have ignored the right way of doing it, as a person might do in calligraphy by merely slapping down the brush, our sitting will have been in vain. We will only be stuck in our own self-styled Zen. Even if we do it for a long time, it will come to nothing.

There are many different ways to study calligraphy. There are also many different books on the subject. However, it is impossible to learn just by reading books and then practicing on your own. If you don't study with a qualified teacher, practicing over and over again the basic strokes as they should be done, you will always be limited to your own self-taught style. This is the same with zazen. I would like you to practice with a true master, someone who can teach you how to do the zazen that is in agreement with the Dharma. I would like you to persevere with sitting until you come to the point that zazen itself is the teacher. Get to the point that zazen will teach itself zazen. It may take some time before you realize that the teacher of zazen is zazen itself, but I would like you to make that effort at all times. Make the effort to continue.

You may be familiar with the following haiku:

I answered that it was
the summer heat—
afterward only tears.

This is a poem written by someone who practices zazen. It expresses the effort that others are unaware of. When he is asked why he looks so thin and tired, he replies that it is due to the summer heat.

Besides that, there is nothing else he can explain. All he can do is shed tears. It is with just such a yearning, reverent spirit that I would like you to endeavor in your search for Zen.

I am very surprised when people become interested in anything that has the word "Zen" attached to it before first finding out whether it is genuine or not. Please don't look for Zen in the wrong place. I caution you again and again not to look outside of yourself. Please practice Zen that is in agreement with the Dharma. Whether we say "the Dharma," or "the Way of Buddha," or "Zen," it always refers to you. Zazen is not brought to a conclusion as a result of going to ask a teacher about it. It must be brought to a conclusion within yourself. Yet to really study your true Self is something that is very difficult. This is because we always look for resolutions somewhere outside of ourselves.

It is a wonderful thing that for some of you the matter is gradually becoming clear. Where is the problem? Please forget about practicing zazen in order to find the solution to the problem. I would like you to understand clearly that zazen is the investigation of the Self. It must be settled within yourself.

"I've come to realize that the eyes lie horizontally and the nose stands vertically. I won't be deceived by others." These are the words of Dogen, and I would like you to remember them. "Others" here doesn't necessarily refer to something outside yourself. It means that you fool yourself. So Dogen is saying, "Don't be fooled even by yourself."

A monk asked, "Why did Bodhidharma come from India to China?" The answer given by the master was, "The oak tree in the garden." At a later time, in response to that reply, Kanzan, a truly wonderful monk, said, "The mind of a thief is hiding in the answer, 'The oak tree in the garden.'" This is a famous story and is said to be the only thing that Kanzan left behind. Indeed, what was the mind or activity of a thief that was hiding there? This is an important question. Please be careful. Please don't be fooled by yourself. Really put life into your zazen. If you are negligent, you will turn into a ghost whose eyes lie vertically and whose nose stands horizontally.

Again, those of you who clearly understand the nature of your zazen, whether it be koan practice, shikantaza, or following the breath, it isn't necessary to listen to what I say. Let go of everything, open yourself up, and be one with your zazen.

I hope you can understand that my only wish for you is that you truly become a person of the Dharma as soon as possible. In both Japan and the West, it seems as if there are many problems that cannot be resolved. In fact, the modern condition seems to be that many, many things cannot be resolved. Things in the world often get stuck within the confines of good and evil, or correct and incorrect. Zen will come to nothing if it cannot go beyond those limits. It is my earnest hope that you will seek for something that transcends good and evil.

GOOD AND EVIL IS TIME; TIME IS NOT GOOD OR EVIL

Regarding the dividing of things into good and evil, Dogen said the following, "Good and evil is time. Time is not good or evil." Nothing is good or evil, neither people nor anything else. This is to say that sometimes there is the thought of good and sometimes the thought of bad. No one can think two thoughts at the same moment. For example, no opposite thoughts such as good and evil, correct and incorrect, can be thought at the same time. If there is a thought of good and it does not disappear, then it is impossible to think of bad. First there is the thought of good, and then the thought of bad.

In that minuscule instant, which changes at lightning speed, the ego-self is created. This is due to the function of consciousness. I will once again explain this matter of consciousness.

Due to the ego-self, we think we are able to think two things at the same time, but this is a mistake. Because of this imaginary ego-self, which essentially does not exist, we constantly view things from the dualistic standpoint of this and that, good and evil. We are twisted and turned about by this ego-self, which is the source of our suffering and delusion.

The Dharma is the relative world of difference. True difference is equality or oneness. In the Dharma, there is neither good nor bad. "This thing" exists regardless of this and that, good and evil, belief and non-belief. It is a condition that is completely beyond comparison. This is why there can be no doubt that if you simply accept things as they are, you will be one with the Dharma.

In Zen Master Dogen's *Fukan-zazengi* are the following words: "Do not interfere with the workings of the mind, nor try to control the movements of your thoughts. Give up the idea of becoming a buddha." This means that we should sit in such a way that we let go of everything and let the functioning of thoughts and perceptions be as they are. The function of the mind is the means by which we perceive things. It gives us the feeling that, in contrast to other things, we are neither wood nor stone.

The function of consciousness is both that of measuring and of discriminating. It also has the function of making assumptions, such as assuming that something exists when in fact it does not. Thoughts are things that are constantly following one another. If there were only one thought, with nothing following it, we couldn't say it was a thought. Thinking is a continuous stream of thoughts. Dogen says we should give up any effort to sit with the intention of stopping at one particular thought or of trying not to think different thoughts. Instead, he emphasizes, we should sit leaving the mind to function as it is.

Daikan Eno (Dajian Huineng) was the Sixth Ancestor of Chinese Zen. He attained enlightenment while he was still a layman, and he later became the successor to Daiman Konin. At the time of his enlightenment he wrote the following verse:

> Huineng has no ways or means
> To cut off the movements of many thoughts.
> The mind is often arising in reaction to conditions,
> How, then, can enlightenment be fostered?

"Huineng has no ways or means." This is to say that he knew nothing about the Buddhadharma or Zen, nor did he have any special ability. "To cut off the movements of many thoughts": he had no thought at all of trying not to think or of trying to leave thoughts as they are. "The mind is often arising in reaction to conditions": in reaction to many different circumstances and conditions, thoughts of liking and disliking are constantly arising. "How, then, can enlightenment be fostered?" He clearly shows there is no means by which enlightenment or the Way can be fostered or increased.

Please compare your present zazen with this verse. I think that perhaps your condition right now is the direct opposite of its meaning. I'd like you to remember this verse, as it will be a good guide for you.

Why is it necessary to take up valuable time with such detailed talk? The reason is that even though you may be doing zazen, due to differences in words and concepts, you simply cannot accept what I say as-it-is. In order to try to get you to understand, it is necessary to divide one thing into many sections, for example: mind, consciousness, thoughts, and perceptions.

Some Zen students practice a kind of zazen called *zuisokkan*. This is a practice whereby, within the form of zazen, you consciously follow the breath. This is not a matter of doing a certain kind of zazen called zuisokkan. The sitting form and following the breath are one thing.

What I say is you must practice them as if they were the same thing. Please stop thinking that the sitting form and following the breath are separate. All thought that takes place within zazen is merely a change in the form of both zazen and zuisokkan.

THE WIND BLOWS EVERYWHERE

For those people whose practice is shikantaza, as soon as you hear "just sit" or practice zazen "single-mindedly," right away you perceive "just," or "single-mindedly," or "as-it-is." Right now, as you see things in front of you, none of these things are in the state of "as-it-is," or "suchness" (shikan). Such words or phrases as "as-it-is" or "suchness" are only explanations that point to reality, to the actual fact. No matter what condition we find ourselves in, it is not possible to be separate from the reality of things-as-they-are. This means that if our intention is to become this state of things as-they-are, the state of suchness, this would be "to put another head on top of the head we already have," a well-known Zen expression.

Through the teaching of Zen, words like *shikantaza* or *zuisokkan* have been created. However, from the standpoint of Buddhism as a whole, it is said that "the true nature of things is without form." If it is not clearly understood that the real form of things is formless, serious mistakes will arise. This is why it must be remembered that the practices of shikantaza or zuisokkan are only "skillful means" that lead to formlessness. Please sit in such a way that you eliminate shikantaza or zuisokkan. Sit so that zazen eliminates shikantaza or zuisokkan. Sit so that zazen itself disappears.

There is an anecdote from the past about a Zen master named Hotetsu who lived on a mountain in China. One summer day, while he was fanning himself, a monk came up and asked, "The nature of the wind is that it constantly blows everywhere. Why, then, are you using a fan?" Hotetsu replied, "You understand the fact that things (the wind) exist, but this is only one side of the matter. You don't know that things also do not exist, and that isn't good." The monk still could not understand, so he asked, "What does it mean that things do not exist?" At that point Hotetsu didn't say anything, but only continued fanning himself quietly.

Often mistakes arise in the direction of your practice because you only know about Zen and know nothing of the Dharma. The Dharma is everywhere and is not the possession of any single person. This means that in order to know the true Self there is no alternative but to become the true Self. Zazen isn't something that a person does. In the same way, it is not a matter of a particular person attaining enlightenment. The world of the Dharma is one in which it is completely impossible for the ego-self to intervene. Please seek the Dharma and remember that this Dharma is without form.

ON EMPTINESS

I would like you to know that all existence is empty. Please also remember that in fact you must not *perceive* this emptiness. There are many different ways to express what we refer to as the Dharma. All expressions such as "suchness," "emptiness," "the Way," and "Zen" point to one thing, the same reality.

For example, when I am in Japan, people refer to me in many different ways, including *"osho-san"* (priest), *"hojo-san"* or *"jushoku-san"* (the resident priest of a temple), *"docho-san"* (abbot), or *"roshi"* (Zen master). Depending on the situation, "this thing" takes on one of these functions. "This thing" functions according to the need of the situation. I think that each one of you is called by different names according to the situation, and each time you answer "Yes" without fail.

In this way, "this thing," which is the coming together of the five *skandhas,* has complete freedom to change according to circumstances. Sometimes we are content, sometimes we are completely dejected. Sometimes we quarrel, sometimes we are happy and at other times sad. We change according to the situation. It is to that extent that "this thing" can act freely. The reason is that "this thing," as well as the situation itself, is completely empty.

Just as *"mu"* (nothingness) is beyond existence and non-existence, we must be careful not to think that *"ku"* (emptiness) is a description of a condition where something that should exist does not. Neither is it the description of a state that, in dualistic terms, is empty in the sense of being vacant or hollow. It is the emptiness of emptiness, it is the emptiness of the circumstances of any situation, and it is the emptiness of yourself.

Why use the word "emptiness"? The reason is that all things, whether with or without form, come about as the result of cause and effect. In connection with the law of cause and effect, we should not make the mistake of thinking that this law has existed absolutely from the beginning. Rather, this law of cause, condition, and result is established as a way to explain the Dharma and emptiness theoretically.

"This thing" is empty. It has no substance, no self-nature, and therefore it is free to change according to circumstances and the situations it encounters. The constantly changing activity of "this thing" is what is referred to as "karma."

THE TEN REALMS

A human being exists in one of the ten realms of delusion and enlightenment. In other words, depending on various conditions, "this thing" lives as a sentient being in one of these ten realms.

What are the ten realms? First of all, there are six realms of suffering and delusion. To continually move around through these six realms is referred to as "transmigration." These six realms are: heaven, human beings, hell, hungry ghosts, animals, and fighting devils *(asuras)*. In the realm of heaven, there is only happiness. It is a condition in which every aspect of life is satisfying. Since this existence is always happy, enjoyable, and wonderful, the situation never arises whereby the teaching of Buddha or any other teaching is sought.

The realm of human beings is a condition in which there is constant change between happiness and sadness, satisfaction and dissatisfaction. The time spent in this realm is said to be shorter than that in any of the other five. However, unless a being lives in this realm, it will have no chance at all to come in contact with the Dharma.

There is a metaphor concerning a blind turtle that symbolizes how extremely rare is the chance to exist even for a short time as a human being. It is a story about a small piece of wood floating in the middle of the ocean. In this piece of wood there is a hole. Once every hundred years, a blind turtle leaves the bottom of the ocean and goes up to the surface to stick its head out of the water. It so happens that the turtle puts its head through the hole in the small piece of wood. This conveys how difficult it is to have the chance to live in the realm of human beings.

Beneath the world of human beings is the realm of hell. Life in this realm is the exact opposite of heaven. Every aspect of this life is a cause of suffering. Due to the excess of pain and suffering, the opportunity for a being in hell to encounter the Buddhadharma does not exist.

The realm of hungry ghosts is one in which it is impossible to become satisfied. The realm of animals is one in which the beings there cannot understand reason, no matter how carefully something is explained to them.

Finally, there is the realm of asuras, or fighting devils, the world of anger. These beings are constantly quarreling and fighting. They want to destroy whatever they see. Of the six realms of delusion, the worst are those of hungry ghosts, animals, and fighting devils. These realms are considered to be even "worse" than hell because they are the easiest realms for human beings to fall into.

We are continually transmigrating through these six worlds. Even today, and even while we are practicing zazen, we are living in one of these realms. This is our reality. A person who is angry, for example, becomes a fighting devil because of that condition. When that condition comes to an end, that person might reflect on the situation and think, "I shouldn't get angry about such a trivial thing." After concluding that it wasn't right to get angry, that person becomes a being who is living in the world of human beings.

In this realm, other thoughts soon arise according to various circumstances. Depending on the nature of those thoughts, there will be constant migration through the other realms. This is all due to the activity of the ego-self, which arises in the minute gap between one thought and the next.

It is said that in the time it takes to snap your fingers there are 900 cycles of birth and death. All things, including "this thing," are changing that quickly. Transmigration through the six realms is also taking place at the same speed. Why don't things remain fixed in certain states? The reason is that there is no substance. This is what is known as "impermanence."

This is the reality of our everyday life. During a meditation retreat, though, the different conditions that we come into contact with are relatively few. It is for that reason that we don't fall into the worst three realms as often. Since we have more time to spend in the realm of human beings, we can carry out our zazen practice.

Once Joshu asked, "What is the Way?" At another time, after his enlightenment, Joshu explained the Way saying, "The Great Way leads to Chang'an [the ancient capital of China]. All ways lead to liberation." The same person was once asking and later teaching. For Joshu himself, there was no change whatsoever. The only difference was the freedom to exist in any of the ten realms. This freedom appeared by forgetting everything, including the ego-self.

So far I have spoken about the six realms of delusion and transmigration through these realms. Apart from these six lower realms there are the four higher realms of *sravakas* (persons who have unshakable confidence in the teaching of Buddha), *pratyeka-buddhas* (self-enlightened buddhas who do not attempt to save others), bodhisattvas, and buddhas. The realms of *sravakas* and *pratyeka-buddhas* are places where belief and that which is believed in still remain. However, since the degree of belief is so strong, beings in these realms do not fall into the realms of delusion.

Above these two realms is the realm of the bodhisattvas. In this realm the purpose of a life is always directed toward other people. Living to help other people means that there is still an object, some other thing, that must be helped. In terms of Zen practice, this outlook could be expressed as "I've realized emptiness, but other things still exist." From the standpoint of Zen, bodhisattvas have still not reached enlightenment.

The highest realm is that of the buddhas. This is the world in which there is nothing to do. There is nothing for a buddha to do. A buddha has no function. A buddha is a being that "has gone beyond all learning." Since there is no thought of helping others, there is no compassion. Since there is no thought of guiding others, there is nothing left to be done.

A buddha is the essence of a thing. In the realm of buddhas, there is only essence. Even in a moment's time, a being in the lowest realm of fighting devils could, on meeting the right conditions, instantly be born into the realm of the buddhas. According to the conditions and circumstances of a situation, it is possible to enter any realm. The reason for this is that all things have no self-nature. They are transient and empty.

Of the ten different realms, the one that people usually search for is heaven. But the fact is that in this realm the heavenly state will surely come to an end. When that condition or good fortune ends, a being will fall from that realm. This means that we must constantly practice in such a way that we encounter the right conditions to become a buddha. Even if we are endowed with the nature to become a buddha but we don't meet the right conditions, we will remain stuck in the delusion of the three worst realms. With one thought, a fighting devil can instantly become a buddha. This is what we refer to as "the teaching of Shakyamuni Buddha," or the principle of cause and effect.

Some people make the mistake of confusing the Buddhist teaching of cause and effect with fatalism. In fact, these two philosophies are completely different. From the viewpoint of fatalism, there is no idea of emptiness or transience. People who are fatalists perceive only that the six realms are real. They think such things as, "In my last life I was in hell and now I've been born into the world of human beings," or "In this life I was born a human being, but because of bad karma I will probably be born in hell in my next life."

When "this thing" is perceived to exist, it is usually thought that when its functions stop, it is dead. In fact, this is not so. Furthermore, the idea that a person's previous life took place before the body was born, or that a person's future life will take place after the body dies, is not the case, either. In Buddhism, transience or the continual change of "this thing" is what is referred to as "life" and "death." When one thought disappears, that is called "death." When the next thought appears, that is called "birth." Thus, we are constantly being born and constantly dying. If something doesn't die, it cannot be reborn. Because something dies, the next thing is born. This is life and death.

Since all of you have had the opportunity to come into contact with Zen, my sincere hope is that you will continue to make the effort to realize the Way of Buddha and become true persons of the Dharma.

Here I would like to introduce a poem by Ryokan, the theme of which is "form is emptiness":

> With no-mind the flower invites the butterfly,
> With no-mind the butterfly reaches the flower.
> The flower doesn't know,
> Neither does the butterfly.
> Not knowing, no knowing—
> Fulfilling the law of the universe.

This is our condition right now, as is all of our everyday life.

THE ONE ARROW OF SEKKYO

Long ago there was a famous hunter by the name of Sekkyo. One day, while out in the mountains, he happened to pass Baso. Baso stopped him and asked, "As you are a master hunter, how many deer can you kill with one arrow?" Sekkyo answered, "No matter how good a hunter is, with one arrow he can only kill one deer at a time." Baso then said, "You are well known as a master hunter, but one doesn't have to be a master hunter to kill one deer at a time with one arrow. With one arrow you should be able to kill a whole herd." Just as Sekkyo turned to glare at Baso, he attained great enlightenment.

Even without knowing about Zen or Buddhism, it is possible in such a way to attain enlightenment. Sekkyo had become so absorbed in his everyday work that, without knowing about Zen or the Dharma, his very life had become samadhi and diligent effort.

Hearing these words of Baso, a Zen master, became the condition by which he attained realization.

If I were to speak of your condition right now, I would say that your zazen practice, your zazen method, is the one arrow of Sekkyo. This arrow is zuisokkan, shikantaza, or koan practice. With this one arrow, then, I would like you to shoot down the whole swarm of delusions and discriminations: the ego-self and No-Self, enlightenment and the deluding passions, and so on—kill them all.

BECOMING YOUR OWN MASTER

Each day Zuigan would admonish himself by calling out to himself, "Master, master!" To call to himself in such a way meant, "Don't be fooled by others!" We are often pulled this way and that by the thoughts and concepts of religion and the everyday world. It is often a problem because you cannot become your own master by yourself. Don't you feel that it is regrettable that you are deceived and fooled by all things, including Shakyamuni Buddha and the sutras, the buddhas and enlightened ones and records of them? On the other hand, if you are not being deceived, then you are indulging in a kind of arrogance based on pride in the ego-self.

Try throwing away both yourself and other things. Isn't that easier and more comfortable? If you don't completely throw away what you have, until now, thought to be common sense, you are still not truly empty. As soon as possible, please become your own master. In fact, it isn't a matter of being deceived by someone else or their words. Don't be fooled by others means that you shouldn't deceive yourself, you shouldn't fool *yourself.*

When Dogen said, "I will not be deceived be others" he had become his own master.

"NO DEPENDENCE ON WORDS AND LETTERS" AND "A SPECIAL TRANSMISSION OUTSIDE THE TEACHINGS"

The teaching of Zen can be characterized by Bodhidharma's expressions "no dependence on words and letters" and "a special transmission outside the teachings." The first expression is often mistakenly interpreted as a rejection of all words and knowledge, or that a person shouldn't even think. This is not what it means. Instead, it means that you cannot truly understand things by using words. The meaning of "a special transmission outside the teachings" is that the real import of Buddha's teaching cannot be found in any of the Buddhist sutras. It is outside any of Buddha's explanations. It is useless, then, to try to look for the real import in the sutras, even if you have understood the meaning of the words. This could be said to be as foolish as waiting for a rabbit to grow horns.

There is absolutely no need to remember what I say in this book. There is no need to try to capture the meanings of the words I use. Yet please continue wholeheartedly with your zazen practice. In that way you can attain liberation, but this will never be possible by merely reading what I say.

STEALING THE FARMER'S COW, SNATCHING THE BEGGAR'S BOWL

It isn't my job to speak on the essence of the Dharma, or to explain what the Dharma is, or to give instruction concerning practice. Instead, my job is to check if what you have attained is correct or not. Someone who merely adopts the form and appearance of a teacher can never be a real guide. If at least once, though, the direction of your practice is clearly settled, there will be no problems. It is for that reason that I speak about different things to you.

The task of a Zen master has been described as "stealing the farmer's cow" or "snatching the beggar's bowl," that is, taking away a person's most important possession. The thought of Zen, the Dharma, the Way of Buddha, your zazen practice, and the idea of yourself—it means taking away all these things. If the farmer's cow or the beggar's bowl is taken away, there is nothing left for them to do. As long as someone is desperately clinging to such things, it is impossible to die the great death, that is, to truly give up your ego-self.

The key to Zen is to keep throwing everything away, no matter how important it may seem. Keep throwing these things away. If a person said to me, "I have nothing left to throw away," I would reply, "Then throw away that 'nothing left to throw away.'" If that person then asked, "But how can I throw away something I don't have?" I would say, "If it is that important, then carry it with you forever." This isn't to say that something is heavy just because you are carrying it. Or that your load will become lighter if you throw something away. I've spoken about this so that you won't be deceived by others. Please reflect on this thoroughly.

As I always say, the functions of the six senses are not dependent on practice or training. They are not the result of the accumulation of experience. Your condition right now is completely without need of any kind of cultivation through practice or training. Whatever you can see, hear, or think, all of this is what we call the true wisdom of Buddha.

This could be your condition at all times if the six sense functions were at one with circumstances in any situation. In this way, as a result of different conditions received by the sense functions, the ego-self disappears. It becomes empty. Please don't be negligent. Maintain your zazen practice with the same amount of tension as Sekkyo when he drew his bow to take aim and before he let loose the arrow. This is the condition of diligent effort. Please continue zazen without being negligent.

EXAGGERATING THE IMPORTANCE OF DOCTRINAL STUDY

As Shakyamuni Buddha began to teach in India, many people were gradually drawn together. Among his disciples were people of very different habits, characteristics, and idiosyncrasies. It was for this reason that the precepts were instituted one at a time, as necessity dictated.

The basis for these different rules was that since the disciples were practicing together as a group, guidelines were needed to keep them from disturbing one another. "As a minimum, let's be careful about these things" was the spirit in which these precepts were born. If practice is not at the center of these precepts, though, they will lose their meaning. In countries where Buddhism formerly flourished, we find now that the precepts are maintained only superficially. This stems from the mistaken understanding that merely observing the precepts is practicing the Way of Buddha.

Buddhist scholarship involves the study of the Tripitaka, the three branches of the Buddhist scriptures. The Tripitaka's function is likened to an explanation of the different properties and effects of a certain medicine. No matter how precise and accurate the description of the efficacy of that wonderful medicine is, just reading the description will not cure the ache in your head or stomach. The zazen we practice is separate from the Tripitaka. It is the special transmission outside of the teachings. Just by practicing zazen we can attain the wisdom of Buddha, without resorting to any other means or procedures. The present state of Buddhism in Japan is that as people's power of perseverance has diminished, the actual practice of zazen has become less and less emphasized. Not only in Japan but in Buddhism in general the trend is for the study of Buddhist doctrine to become of sole importance.

Every morning we chant the *Sankiraimon* (Taking Refuge in Buddha, the Dharma, and the Sangha). In that short text are the following words: "I take refuge in the Dharma and vow together with all sentient beings to enter the storehouse of the sutras, the wisdom of which is as deep and vast as the ocean." This means that through study of the Tripitaka we will attain learning that is as deep and vast as the ocean. But this is like only one wheel on a cart. A cart cannot move with just one wheel. Zen is the other wheel. When the balance of these two wheels is well maintained, then we can say the Dharma flourishes. Please think of Zen as only one small window through which you can get a glimpse of the Dharma.

The fact is, though, that you won't understand unless you study the Buddhist teachings and listen to what I have to say at least once. If you don't, it will be as if you are sailing on the ocean without a chart. You will have no idea which way to go or how to get to your destination. That is why I talk to you, even though essentially it isn't really necessary.

VERIFICATION FOR ONESELF AND CERTIFICATION BY A MASTER

Imagine that there is an island in the ocean that is said to be uninhabited. You will never know if people are living there or not unless you actually go there. Even though someone has told you that the island is uninhabited, you don't believe it. Perhaps there are some people who, when hearing the same statement, would agree, but this would be nothing more than blind belief. Since you haven't actually seen it for yourself, it cannot be said to be the real thing. You believe, but there is still a tinge of doubt and dissatisfaction remaining.

Then one day you cross over to that island, and by doing so you actually prove that the island is indeed uninhabited. This is Zen. In return, another person who has already crossed over to that island will verify the fact of your having crossed over to see it. He will give you a certificate that reads, "Without a doubt you have been to see the uninhabited island." This is what is called "*inka shomei*" or certification of realization. The custom of a master certifying his disciple in this way is characteristic only of the Zen sect.

I myself received such a certification from my teacher saying I have been to that uninhabited island. This was also the way I certified my teacher. In the case of Shakyamuni Buddha, there was no one preceding him who could certify his attainment. Who, then, certifies Shakyamuni Buddha? It is his disciple who gives the certification. It is at that point he first becomes one with Shakyamuni Buddha.

THE CERTIFICATION OF TRUE PEACE OF MIND

What does it mean to say that a person has attained true peace of mind, has attained freedom, and has awakened to the true Self? It is the clear realization that before that attainment there was never any reason to suspect that there was delusion or anxiety or any restriction of freedom. It is to realize that from the beginning none of these things existed. This is what is called "enlightenment," or "liberation," meaning "to liberate" or "save" yourself. If practice is thought to be a process by which the elements of anxiety and delusion are eliminated, this is a mistake.

As I have said many times, the condition of things as-they-are, or *shikan*, is something that exists prior to practice. Expressions such as "everything is all right as-it-is" or "shikantaza" would not have come to be used if a person had to rely on practice as the means to be saved from anxiety or lack of freedom and it wasn't possible to attain true peace of mind. A person who has attained true freedom describes that condition as one where "things are as-they-are," but, in fact, there is no such condition, and expressions such as *"things are as-they-are,"* or *"suchness"* (shikan) are nothing more than descriptions.

On hearing the expression *"things are as-they-are,"* a person who has not attained that freedom perceives that such a condition exists where "things are as-they-are." This does not mean that by doing so something objective is being perceived. Instead, it means that the ego-self exists. To perceive something, to think that something exists, is to perceive the ego-self. At that time, the ego-self can be said to exist.

■ TO STUDY THE WAY IS TO STUDY THE SELF

Without being aware of it, you have come to perceive "this thing" as yourself. That you have done this for a long time poses a big problem. "This thing" belongs to no one. If, in fact, "this thing" were you, the word "you" would itself become unnecessary. "This thing," which you don't really understand, can clearly perceive on seeing or hearing something. That it can perceive or be conscious of something is the reason that delusion arises. Delusion arises at that point because there is both that which is understood and that which is not understood. It is mistaken to think something exists that, in fact, does not exist. This is the case with the ego-self, which though it does not exist, is thought to be "you." Since "this thing," which is not really understood, is perceived to exist, when things don't go as you wish, they become the cause of feelings of dissatisfaction or lack.

Accordingly, Dogen had this to say:

> To study the Way is to study the Self.
> To study the Self is to forget the ego-self.
> To forget the ego-self is to be enlightened by all things.
> To be enlightened by all things is to cast off body and mind both
> of oneself and others.

Dogen is asking you to look at "this thing" that you perceive to be yourself and then to ask yourself, "What is the true Self? Who *am* I anyway?" He is saying that to pursue and investigate these questions is the practice of the Way of Buddha. "This thing" is nothing more than a symbol of you. If you can just forget "this thing," this symbolic ego-self, the division between it and other things will disappear. "To cast off" means that "this thing" becomes one with all things, that the body and mind of yourself as well as others have been cast off. All things have disappeared, they have become empty. It is the realization that already everything has been cast off, that everything is one and already empty. It is not a matter of *becoming* one, becoming "*Mu*" (nothingness), or becoming "*ku*" (emptiness) as a result of practice.

LETTING GO OF ONENESS

In order that you don't misunderstand, I would like you to remember that it is not possible for just one thing to exist. On becoming empty or becoming one with something, or on casting off body and mind, at that moment all things have ceased to exist. If, on becoming one with all things, something still exists—for example, something that perceives or realizes the nature of emptiness or nothingness or enlightenment—this means that there is something that hasn't completely become one. We could say that only that thing perceiving in such a way exists outside of enlightenment.

By means of the study of doctrine, it is possible to explain this matter of becoming one. Even in religions other than Buddhism, it is taught that all things are one and that true peace of mind cannot be realized without becoming this oneness. But this oneness must be cast off.

If a person doesn't come to Zen, in the end she or he will never come to the point of letting go of oneness. She or he won't be able to let go of the ego-self, yet it must be cast off. Nevertheless, your condition right now is unmistakably a condition where everything has fallen away. Right now you are making a great effort to do *this* or not to do *that*, but I would like you to know that this problem itself is empty. This is the practice of Zen.

THE FIRST STEP ON THE WAY

The practice of the Way of Buddha begins from the point of awakening to the true Self. You may think that before that happens you are practicing the Way, but it can be said that you are still not one with it. I want you to understand that until you awaken to the true Self, whatever you have heard and come to know about Shakyamuni Buddha's teaching of emptiness is solely from the standpoint of the ego-self. If you cannot accept this, a serious obstacle will arise in your practice. That is why I would like you to awaken to the true Self as soon as possible in order to make that first step forward on the Way.

If we teachers are too helpful or too careful in everything we do, it is said that it will have a harmful effect. When you arrive at a meditation retreat, ample preparations have been made. All you have to do is enter a *samadhi* of zazen and that will be enough. My only worry is that since everything is so well organized, the result might be that the will to make an effort, to be diligent, will be weakened.

If your determination is very strong, zazen itself will be enough for you. No such words as these will be necessary. In Zen, this is what is referred to as "resolution of faith," a strong, unshakable belief. With this attitude, if you really endeavor in zazen, you will surely awaken to the true Self. However, there are others here who still cannot completely devote themselves to zazen because they don't understand the theory behind zazen. It is for those who feel they cannot enter Zen without a more detailed explanation that I will say more. But please remember, it is a mistake to think that you can reach what is real by thought or as a process of refining your thought.

■ THE PROBLEM WITH SHIKANTAZA

For some time there have been teachers in Japan, the United States, and Europe who have taught that it is a mistake to have a goal in the practice of zazen. This is the way most people think of Zen these days. These teachers, though, are mistaken. The reason is that they don't know that perception arises after the fact, *after* the reality. They set up the idea of not having a goal *beforehand*. They think that zazen is a condition where you need not do or think anything. They think it is reality itself. They think that because the thought exists, the reality also exists. But it is clear that even if you sit for many years this way, there will always be a feeling of something missing.

The condition that is variously described as "*shikan*," "*as-it-is*," "*suchness*," or "*nothing to realize, nothing to attain*" is something that comes before perception. Therefore, when those teachers say that you should not have a goal, and tell people to just "*do shikantaza*" which is "*just sit single-mindedly*," the problem is that the person who hears that instruction perceives "just" or "sit single-mindedly." In this way, he or she practices zazen within the thought of shikan, or "just sitting." By doing this, the person will never become one with shikan. To do this kind of zazen means it will never come to completion. That there is no completion means that Zen and sitting will never disappear. It is a condition in which you are attached to Zen. You cannot be free of it. As long as anything like "sitting," or "Zen," or "practice" exists even in the slightest degree, you will never be able to find true satisfaction.

What is referred to as *shikan* is the fact. It is reality. That which is referred to as reality is something that cannot be perceived. "The true nature of things is formless." This is what we call *shikan*. This means that it is a mistake to create shikan within your own thoughts and perceptions. Perception comes after the fact. Please understand this.

THE PROBLEM WITH KOAN ZEN

Next, let us consider Zen in which there *is* a goal. *Zen* in which enlightenment, or *kensho* (seeing into your true nature), is the goal is called "koan Zen." This is a type of Zen where koans are solved one by one, as if you are climbing a ladder. By doing this, it seems as if enlightenment is gradually deepened. If a person perceives these steps and looks for something outside of his condition right now, it is uncertain whether the ultimate end will be reached, even though he is practicing zazen. There will also be the constant worry that there might be another level, and this means that you must continue to look.

At the time when Dogen went to China, koan Zen was widespread. Dogen keenly felt there was an error implicit in koan Zen, that it is the sickness of "glimpsing wisdom." Many people have had only a small glimpse and then been told by a master whom they trust that their little glimpse was *kensho* or *satori*—enlightenment—and then they don't penetrate further, penetrate all the way. In Japan as well, there have been many abuses of koan Zen. As I just mentioned, often after a small experience, a teacher will tell the student that he or she has "forgotten the self" and approve the student's *kensho*. The teacher will then present the student with koan after koan and this mistaken notion will be perpetuated. It is regrettable that there are so many mistaken masters like this.

Koans themselves are neither good nor bad, shallow nor deep. At the same time, with regard to the different types of zazen practice like shikantaza and so on, there is neither correct zazen nor mistaken zazen. If there is wrong understanding on the teacher's part, this will cause serious mistakes for the student. It is the equivalent of pointing a person west when he or she wants to go east. For many people who claim to have experienced kensho, there remains a person, a self, who perceives this thing called kensho. There is someone remaining who is cognizant of having had such an experience. Which only means that that person, that self who is perceiving kensho, or enlightenment, is in fact outside of enlightenment. As the perceiving self remains, the enlightenment isn't yet the real thing. As long as there is a self that perceives such a thing, there can be no reason to expect it is real. Also, the effect of such an experience is of having "had kensho," i.e., all suffering, delusion, and distracting thoughts are said to disappear. This means, though, that a gap, or division, will arise between "before" and "after" the experience.

USING THE FORM OF ZEN AS AN EXPEDIENT

The teaching of Shakyamuni Buddha in the form of Zen as it has been transmitted from India through China to Japan is different from either of the two approaches I have just discussed. The difference is that the condition right now is one in which all things, including the Dharma, are empty, and where even emptiness itself does not exist.

This is to say that there is nothing that needs to be called "Zen," or "practice," or "the Dharma." The condition right now is as-it-is and cannot be perceived at all. As there is nothing to look for, there is nothing to throw away.

The gap between delusion and enlightenment is created in accordance with whether the fact of reality is perceived or not. To perceive that reality exists is called "delusion." To experience directly that reality does not exist is called "enlightenment." This fact of "right now" is what Master Nansen—when he explained "everyday mind is the Way" to Joshu—called "neither knowing nor not knowing." I would really like you to understand that our condition right now is completely beyond all perception, including delusion and enlightenment.

In both streams of Zen mentioned above, it is the forms of Zen, whether shikantaza or koan, that become the goal. For many people who practice shikantaza, *not to have a goal* becomes the goal itself. This is an error that arises because they only know about Zen without knowing about the Dharma. It is the Dharma that must be sought. But the Dharma itself is something that can neither be perceived nor has any form. When Master Rinzai was about to die, he said that he would transmit the Dharma to someone who had extinguished it.

It is possible to use either of these two types of zazen—shikantaza or koan—as an expedient means to reach the Dharma. If it is understood that these forms of zazen are not the end in themselves but rather part of the process, then there is no problem. In any event, if you do not rely on *some* method, you will never arrive at true understanding.

When I give you instruction, I may say, "do shikantaza" or "concentrate on this koan," or "follow the breath." These are crutches that you use until you can walk freely. It is said that practice without practice is true practice. Or zazen without zazen is true zazen.

This means that at the moment you really become one with sitting it-self, sitting has disappeared. When shikantaza truly becomes *shikan*, shikan disappears. To say that the koan has been resolved or come un-tangled means to have become one with the koan at that moment. The koan has disappeared. This means that things with form must be elim-inated or extinguished. This is what is called "seeking the Dharma."

At other times I have spoken of using something bad to treat an ill-ness, meaning to control poison with poison. Illness can be cured even with a poisonous drug. What I wanted to say was that depending on the way something is used, the result can be good or bad. With regard to having a goal, if we take a person who is thirsty, for example, he has the urgent objective of drinking a cup of water. When he drinks the water, at that instant there is no longer an objective. Thus, the act of drinking the water is both the means and the end. My intention in speaking about all this is not to criticize anything by saying "this is good" or "this is bad." My heartfelt hope is only that you can attain peace of mind and true satisfaction. This is certainly possible if you come to realize that "everything is all right as-it-is now," and that there was never anything to look for and nothing to throw away.

THE CONDITION RIGHT NOW

Your condition where there is nothing to be sought for and nothing to be thrown away exists right now, regardless of whether you have awakened to the true Self or not. My own condition is one where there is no Dharma, no Zen, and I am not looking for the Way. There is neither diligence nor laziness, nor is there delusion. I have no in-tention of trying to grasp something or get rid of something.

I am always thinking of something. When I see something beauti-ful, I think it's beautiful. When I don't like something, I don't like it. When something is disagreeable, it's disagreeable. It is the same for everything. I think about things of tomorrow, of one month from now, and of one year from now. Things of the past exist within memories. Essentially, both the past and future exist by means of thought. This is my condition right now. If I were to speak on the subject of the present moment and to explain it, that is what I would say.

Those of you who think you would like to realize this for yourselves should do zazen as I have instructed you. Another thing I would like to remind you is that in principle the true Self is something that essentially cannot be perceived.

WHAT IS CONSCIOUSNESS?

We were conceived as a result of sexual union between our father and mother. In Buddhism, that moment of conception is called *consciousness*. At that very moment, form appears. During the next twenty-eight weeks, the six sense functions as well as our gender develop. This all happens as a result of cause and conditions. It could not happen with only the cause or only the conditions. Intrinsically, it is due to the nature of causes and conditions and effects that the six sense functions and the differences between male and female develop. Those functions are brought about by various contributory factors. They have only come together in this way, and nowhere is there an essence or a center. There is no you, no ego-self, no true Self. After a period of about nine months, a newborn child is delivered from its mother's womb. We call this a baby, but the baby itself doesn't know it's a baby or even a human being. The sensation of feeling and receiving is first experienced when the baby is born. Sometime later it begins to discriminate between pleasant and unpleasant. This is not a matter of understanding this difference. Those sensations simply exist. In other words, functions such as liking or disliking, or feeling something is painful or pleasurable, merely exist.

Among these different functions is one of attachment. It isn't that this attachment has a certain objective. Rather, there is only the function of attachment itself. This function, then, gives rise to the function of wanting to touch or take something or of wanting to make something one's own. This isn't the function of a certain person. It is simply the function of the wish to take hold of something.

The strongest attachment is the attachment to life. This is a function of the consciousness that arose at the time of conception. This is the result of our condition from the time of birth. It is the nature of our ignorance, of our delusion. There are only the six sense functions. There is nothing that can be perceived as you or "me." These six senses are not the functions of an individual person. It is a condition just like that of any other animal or plant, where there are only the functions themselves. This physical body that we can see with our eyes is called "form."

Mental activity is composed of sensation, perception, formation, and consciousness. We are made up of the coming together of these five *skandhas:* form, sensation, perception, formation, and consciousness. Without *the function of form,* the mental functions would not arise. This is why we cannot think of the physical body as being separate from mental activity. This is also why, as I mentioned earlier, no matter how much you refine thought, that in itself cannot comprise everything.

A question that is frequently asked is whether the physical body or mental activity comes first. In fact, they arise at the same time. The physical body receives impressions from the outside environment through the six senses. Simultaneously, on receiving these impressions, many different conditions arise as a result of mental activity.

Nothing is comprised of only one thing.

While the true Self may seem something special, it really isn't. As I have just explained, it is merely knowing the fact that only the functions exist. These functions themselves are what is called the Dharma. It is to realize that the Dharma is you yourself. This reality is expressed as *"the true Self."*

If you think that by awakening to the true Self it will be possible to make various correct or pure decisions vis-à-vis your everyday life in society, I would like you to realize that this way of thinking is mistaken. The main point of practice is to investigate and then discern the nature of *consciousness*, the last of the five skandhas.

I would like you to realize that while consciousness raises all kinds of delusions and fantasies, it is also the means by which we can attain the Way of Buddha. By thoroughly investigating consciousness and realizing that it is empty, it is possible to reach the condition of great satisfaction.

I have just explained many things, but in the end I would like you to understand that ultimately everything is empty, that all things arise only through cause and effect. Because human beings as well as all things come about through cause and effect, there is no substance or essence. Nothing is comprised of merely one thing, so there is no center or nucleus. There is no way for just any one thing to exist by itself, and this is what is called *"emptiness."* All things are said to be empty, but please remember that *emptiness* is only a tentative explanation and that, in fact, this *emptiness* cannot be perceived.

THE LIGHT OF THE DHARMA, THE LIGHT WITHIN YOURSELF

What is it that we refer to as the Way? To explain this, I would like to mention the following:

> Being is conceived in the womb,
> Becoming a person takes place in the world,
> Seeing is done with the eyes,

Hearing is done with ears,

Smelling is done with the nose,

Speaking is done with the mouth,

Carrying is done with the hands,

Walking is done with the feet.

This is what is called buddha-nature.

This is the answer given by Bodhidharma (before he left India for China) to King Iken's question, "What is the Way?" It is said that on hearing these words King Iken was suddenly enlightened. This is what is called Zen, or "the Dharma," or "the Way of Buddha." It is completely your condition right now. There is nothing other than this condition, and that is the import of these words.

At the end of his life Shakyamuni Buddha said, "Move on with the light of the Dharma. This is the light of yourself. Proceed with it and don't look elsewhere." This was his instruction to his disciples.

If I were to say what the aim or goal of practice should be, I would say "zazen is zazen." I would like you to make an effort so that that would simply be enough. This doesn't only refer to the sitting form of Zen, or zazen. It means to practice each thing, each activity for its own sake. In your work and your daily life, each activity is the end in itself. In this way there is no special significance attached to anything. During the past five days, I think I have only served to deepen your confusion. It is as if I have cultivated your knowledge of Zen with a hoe. Let "zazen is zazen" be the new seed. There is none better. If what I have said has been confusing for you, please don't think badly of me.

AWAKENING TO THE CHAOS WITHIN YOU

The following story comes from China. It concerns a man named Konton (konton is the Japanese word for chaos or confusion) and is a parable that demonstrates how the essence of something was destroyed.

Konton's head was as smooth as an egg. His face had none of the orifices that ordinary people have. Two men were much indebted to Konton. In order to show their gratitude, they decided to carve one hole in his head each day over a seven-day period. In doing so, they thought they would make Konton's head look like theirs. When they were finished, they were sure that Konton would be happy with their efforts. But, in fact, when they asked him how he felt, they found he was dead.

The point of this story is that these men had, by meddling with something, destroyed its very nature. Even though they had meant to be helpful, they ended up taking his life. In the same way, we meddle with the Konton inside ourselves. I would like you to be aware of that. I would like it to be that as a result of zazen practice, your efforts are not in vain. Please don't try to grasp something that is not the true essence of the true Self. I would like you to understand that, in awakening to the true Self, there is nothing to be proud of. Or even if there is great confusion, there is nothing to be anxious about. It is to that degree that Zen is not something special.

THE LAW OF CAUSE AND EFFECT

In each place, at each moment, I would like you to continue living your life and entrusting yourself to cause and effect as-it-is. With absolutely no feeling of either satisfaction or dissatisfaction, abandon yourself to conditions as they arise. To abide serenely within these conditions is what is called "the life of Zen."

Your condition right now is already the result. This means that this result was undoubtedly brought about by a corresponding cause in the past. One second before, ten minutes before, one day before, ten years before—all are the past. The condition at present is the cause of what will happen in the future. The future is an extension of the present. If your present condition is not so desirable, then you must quickly try to change the cause. Otherwise, your condition tomorrow, the day after tomorrow, or ten years from now will be exactly the same as your condition right now.

This applies to you individually as well as to the problems of the world. The present state of confusion in the world did not come about by chance. There was definitely a past cause. The principle of cause and effect does not allow the interference of the ego-self. If only one or two people who really understand the law of cause and effect came forward, it would help to point the world in a good direction. This is urgently required.

The ideal of Buddhism is to enter Nirvana, to attain enlightenment. This is the ideal, and it is because many people have accomplished this that we can now follow the same way of zazen. Please become this very person. It is not enough just to understand the teaching intellectually. Through the practice of Zen, it is definitely possible to become "this very person." I would like you to believe that and make the necessary effort to do it.

Whatever we do in our daily life, it is for the sole purpose of attaining the Way. For this, we take care of our health and pay attention to what we eat. I would like you to keep in mind the goal of attaining the Way by forgetting the ego-self, whether in your life at home or at work.

In closing, I would like to introduce a poem by So Toba:

Rozan famous for its misty mountains,
Sekko for its water.
Before going it was a matter of much regret.
Later I went and returned.
Nothing special.
The misty mountains of Rozan,
The water of Sekko.

PART IV
ELEMENTS IN THE PRACTICE OF ZEN

THE FUNCTIONS OF THE BODY, SPEECH, AND THOUGHT

One big mistake made by many people concerning zazen is thinking that it is limited to the form of sitting. Actually, all functions of the body, speech, and thought must be zazen. Zazen of the body refers to the posture of sitting straight, crossing the legs, and holding the hands together. Zazen of speech includes the words we use during the day, seasonal or morning greetings, chanting the Heart Sutra during the morning sutra service, the verses chanted before eating, and the various words used throughout the day. Lastly, zazen of thought is the functioning of the mind, something that we cannot see. Thinking various ideas, planning, devising, deluding discrimination, random thoughts, and so on, all movements of the mind are zazen.

On saying, then, that all functions of the body, speech, and thought are zazen, it is easy to fall into the trap of thinking, "Why is it necessary to do zazen or seek something by means of Zen?" The problem here with thinking "all activities are zazen" is that we know it by means of learning. It is merely intellectual understanding. Since the reality "now" is divided in two—subject and object—the thought arises that there is no need to do zazen. We must be careful about this.

THE PROBLEM OF THE SELF THAT KNOWS

In the beginning, Zen Master Dogen had a question, which can be expressed in the following way: "The teaching of Buddhism is that this body itself is Buddha. Essentially, a human being is Buddha, the Dharma, and Zen. Why, then, is it necessary to practice?" As there were no teachers in Japan who could resolve this question for him, he went to seek the answer in China. After a long period and many hardships, he finally met Zen Master Nyojo, and then "cast off body and mind." At that time he said:

> The eyes lie horizontal,
> The nose stands vertical.
> I will not be deceived by others.
> The Buddhadharma does not exist in the least.

"Willows are green, flowers are red." Or "all human beings are endowed with buddha-nature." Or "all beings are essentially Buddha itself, are Zen itself." Dogen said unequivocally that there is no mistake in these statements either before or after "body and mind cast off."

From the vantage point of the Dharma, everything is empty. There is no need to "cast off body and mind." We are already within that state of freedom. So why, then, can't you accept all phenomena as they are? The only major problem lies in whether, in the activities of seeing, hearing, experiencing, and knowing, the ego-self intervenes or whether it has completely disappeared. It is because of the intervention of the ego-self that you cannot accept things as they are. This is something I would really like you to be aware of. It is in order to completely wash away the intervention of the ego-self that zazen is so necessary.

Many people mistakenly think: "What I'm now observing and experiencing is my real self. To forget that self or to accept another true Self is unnecessary." This is how most people think. Others, on perceiving the self as an object, think: "I must let the self drop away. The ego-self must be let go of." If you think this way, please understand that it is a serious mistake.

As I mentioned earlier, all beings and all phenomena of the world (mountains, rivers, grass, and trees) are composed of the four elements—earth, water, fire, and air. These elements have no fixed center; they freely change according to circumstances. However, if "I" is fixed as a sort of center or source, then it is no longer possible to change freely anymore. Fixing the "I" in this way is the source of delusion. And because "I" is perceived as existing, the deluding thought arises that there must be something that is the source.

In the beginning, Shakyamuni Buddha also thought that there must be something that is the source or origin of suffering. This was the reason he began to practice. But on seeing the morning star, that is, on realizing enlightenment, he knew that there was no source of suffering. In other words, all things arise because of conditions and all things disappear for the same reason. He realized that all phenomena are produced by causation (Jap.: *engi*; Skt.: *pratitya-samutpada*). In order to explain causation, Shakyamuni built a "phantom castle" and named the castle "emptiness."

Emptiness is an explanation of oneness, where there is not the slightest gap for the opinions of the ego-self to enter. Please consider emptiness as a condition where all concepts have been taken away. The quickest way to be free of such deluding opinions is Zen. It is unnecessary to repeat this, but I would like you to remember that zazen is all the activities of the body, speech, and thought. I often use words like "Zen," or "the Dharma," or "the Way." Please remember that these are all references to the same thing.

THREE ESSENTIAL ELEMENTS OF ZAZEN PRACTICE

Those of you who are at present practicing and studying Zen with another roshi should not come to consult with me about your zazen experience. The reason is the danger of confusion. I would like you to understand that it is wrong to think the teaching of everyone called "roshi" is the same, or that anyone by that title is a suitable teacher. However, if you have any doubts about what you have been taught with regard to practice, or if you have doubts about religion in general and so on, then you are welcome to come to see me.

There are three elements you cannot do without in Zen practice: asking a master about the Dharma; the practice of zazen; and observing the precepts. The objective of Zen practice is to graduate as quickly as possible from zazen and return to the time before you knew anything about zazen.

Some people become intoxicated with zazen and in this way lose sight of their real Self. They mistakenly fall into the habit of thinking that they are doing zazen wholeheartedly. Such people are a long way from true Zen practice.

Others mistakenly teach that zazen is very good for your whole life and simply ask people to sit. However, if zazen is not free of all viewpoints such as good and bad, it isn't the real thing. It is all right, though, to take time off from your busy life and work in order to develop your powers of concentration by absorbing yourself wholeheartedly in Zen practice.

With regard to the first element—asking a master about the Dharma—Zen Master Dogen had the following advice for people who don't know what to do if they cannot find a true master. He cautioned them strictly, saying, "In such a case it is best to stop practicing temporarily. There is less danger in quitting than in practicing in a mistaken manner." The reason is that practicing is like crossing the ocean without a chart; there is always the danger of unknown reefs.

Concerning the second element, the practice of zazen, it is less dangerous for those who have no master to devote themselves to their work instead of doing zazen in a mistaken way. Simply lose yourself in your work and become engrossed in it.

The last essential element is observing the precepts. This involves leaving all things as they are, without interfering or imposing your own opinions on the way things are. If you are free from your ideas, then the precepts are already observed even before you intend to do so. Why is it necessary to do things the way they have been decided? All things have laws or principles that govern them. To observe the precepts is to follow those laws. Observing the precepts means that all things are one and there is no way to interfere with that oneness. A person who can live life following these laws or rules, whose life is in accordance with these laws, is a buddha.

This is a life in which cause and result are one.

If you sit for a long time, your legs will gradually begin to hurt. No matter how long a person has been sitting or how much experience he or she has, there will always be times when your legs hurt. The only difference, though, is whether or not you lose your zazen method because of the pain. It isn't good if the pain in your legs stops you from practicing. In that case, you and zazen are two separate things. You must be able to leave the pain in your legs as-it-is and still be able to do zazen properly.

When the power of zazen is weak, you end up going off in the direction of whatever condition arises. But when the power of zazen is strong, no matter what arises, zazen is right there. It is easy to realize the Way if you sit like that.

The practice of Zen is the study of the Self. It isn't a matter of following the words of some Zen master, whether written or spoken. I would like you not to be mistaken on this point. Don't look for Zen in the Buddhist teachings or in the words of a teacher. The role of a teacher is to keep a person going in a straight line in the study of the Self.

THROWING AWAY YOUR STANDARDS

The key to Zen is that no matter how important something is, it must be thrown away. Keep on throwing and throwing and throwing away your standards. The following story illustrates how one man threw away all the opinions he had been using as standards.

Noh is one of the traditional drama forms of Japan. This story concerns a Noh actor named Konparu Zenchiku (1405—70?), who made a great effort to practice zazen and later received certification of his realization from his master. He expressed the condition of having forgotten the ego-self (the condition in which all standards have been thrown away) in this way: "No matter how I look at it, there is nothing blacker than snow."

His master said, "If you understand that, then all is well," and he gave him the certification.

You may be deeply cultured and have considerable knowledge. Nonetheless, I would like you to forget all your standards just once. Then you will be able to use them in a more meaningful way. My only wish is for you to throw away the standards you have had until now, and later you will be able to use them in a more vital way. If you are free from any viewpoint, then you live for the sake of the Dharma.

GREAT DILIGENCE

There is a story of an earnest Zen practitioner who each evening before going to bed would say to himself, "Today my zazen has *again* ended in the same way. How will zazen go tomorrow?" Every night, he would tearfully reflect on the condition of his zazen and in this way encourage himself in the practice of Zen. Usually he would go to bed at nine or ten o'clock, but one night he went outside to sit quietly instead. After some time he realized his clothes were completely soaked. He felt cold and wet, and he thought, "When did I come to sit? When did it start to rain so that my clothes became wet?" It was to that extent that he had been one with his zazen. This is an example of being completely concentrated on one thing. Concentrating means to sit so single-mindedly that you forget you are doing zazen. I would like you to try to sit this way.

Each of you is doing the kind of zazen most suitable for you. Some people are sitting *shikantaza,* others are doing koan practice, some are following the breath, still others are counting breaths. Please make the effort to be one with your zazen.

As human beings we have the habit of thinking. Thinking is nothing but a habit. In order to be free of this habit, it is necessary to practice zazen. If the power of zazen is strong, the habit of thinking becomes weak, and then you can really concentrate on your zazen. In contrast, if the habit of thinking is strong, then the power of zazen becomes weak. In that case, zazen is split into two—the consciousness of the ego-self and zazen.

In the *Sandokai* (Harmony of Difference and Equality) sutra are the following words, "Merging with principle is still not enlightenment." No matter how completely you understand the essence or principle, it is still not true enlightenment or liberation. There are people who are bound hand and foot by the rope of principle, which is something they cannot see. In order to cut this rope, it is necessary at times to rely on the practice of following the breath, or koan practice, or *shikantaza.* If you don't do this, it will not be possible to cut the binding rope. Please absorb yourself in your zazen practice. That is all I ask of you.

"WHAT IS THE WAY"

One day a monk asked his master, "What is the Way?" The monk was asking about the Way of Buddha. In a broad sense, you can also understand the Way to mean "the ultimate," "the mind of peace and freedom," or "the Truth." The master replied, "Everyday mind is the Way."

The words "everyday mind" express the condition of our lives free of our own ideas and opinions. Washing one's face, brushing one's teeth, talking, taking meals, working—all these activities take place before thought. This was the point of the master's answer. He told the monk that *that* was what he was looking for.

There is the expression "to create waves when there is no wind." What does this mean? To the monk's question, "What is the Way?" the master answered, "Everyday mind is the Way." When you hear this, you might look at your life and think, "Ah! This condition now is 'everyday mind.' Our life itself is the Way. So that is what is meant by 'the Way.'" In this manner you insert your own ideas by looking at the condition of your life. In other words, it is a condition of being conscious of or perceiving something. If you leave it this way, then there is no wind to make waves. On hearing an explanation of the Way, you think, "Yes, of course! This is the Way." By perceiving something that it isn't possible to perceive, you create waves.

The monk was told by his master, "Everyday mind is the Way. Every aspect of your life is the Way." But the monk simply could not accept that answer. Why? Because he had been practicing zazen single-mindedly for a long time. He could accept that fire is hot, water is cool, salt is salty, and sugar is sweet. Yet he was not at peace simply knowing these things, and for that reason he had been earnestly doing zazen. Then he asked the following question, "I don't understand what you mean by 'everyday mind is the Way.' How can I understand 'everyday mind'? What sort of practice should I do in order to understand it?" The master replied, "If you seek for it, you will go in the wrong direction." If you set up Zen, or the Way, or the Truth, or the true Self as being separate from yourself, and then seek for them and try to understand them, in the end you will only distance yourself farther from the Way.

Seeing things as they are, or hearing things without resistance, or accepting things as they are—no matter how purely and innocently we may do all these—they in fact take place within the consciousness of the ego-self. In seeing, or hearing, or accepting simply and purely, already the viewpoint of the ego-self has formed. The condition preceding the appearance of your own ideas is already the condition in which you accept things and hear things as-they-are. In other words, it is a reality where you are one with things. This is what you must seek for.

The monk asked again, "If I never seek for it, how can I ever understand the Way?" The master replied, "The Way is neither knowing nor not knowing. Knowing is illusion, not knowing is indifference." The monk who was asking these questions was Joshu. After he made "everyday mind is the Way" his own, he said, "Before I was used by time, but after I had truly understood 'everyday mind,' I was able to use time." This is being free of the consciousness of the ego-self, forgetting the ego-self, becoming the Way itself.

We are all just like Joshu, people in the midst of the Way. So please realize that the Way is you yourself. This is what I would like you to do. By realizing the Way, each of you will resurrect Joshu.

THE SICKNESS OF BEING ATTACHED TO EMPTINESS

In Buddhism we use the expressions "emptiness" *(ku)* and "nothingness" *(mu)*. When I speak of "blank time," I don't mean that it is a condition where there is nothing or that it is completely empty. Rather it is a condition where everything is fully present, where everything is as it should be. It is a condition where nothing bothers anything else, where things are harmonious. This is what we call "emptiness" in Buddhism. If we think about emptiness or nothingness in a conceptual way, it is easy to get the impression that something that has been full and complete until now suddenly drops out of sight and disappears. It seems as if it is only that thing that has become empty and has disappeared.

People who do zazen within their own ideas create an image of "emptiness," or an image of "nothingness." They create these images themselves. They convince themselves that these images are what is expressed in Buddhism as "emptiness" and "nothingness." Then they practice zazen inside these images. This is a very big mistake.

Among the Japanese who have been practicing zazen for a long time are some who fall into the error of a conceptual understanding of emptiness and nothingness. Eventually this understanding becomes the basis for mistaken ways of thinking, such as, "I won't get caught up in things. I won't let things bother me." Or "whatever happens is the Way itself." There are people who mistakenly teach Zen like this. This is a grave error. It isn't Zen, it isn't the Way of Buddha, and it isn't the Dharma. For people who think like this, their life is nothing but sadness and fear, in other words, it is nihilistic. In order to escape from that condition, they must constantly keep busy doing some activity. Things end up like that for them.

People who misunderstand "emptiness" and "nothingness" cannot understand the blank time at our tea ceremonies. They shouldn't understand this time in a nihilistic way. Yet when they ask, "Why is there this blankness?" there is a danger they will completely misunderstand this matter. This is something I would like you to be very careful about.

THE NATURE OF ZEN

I would like to introduce a verse written by a man who found enlightenment through the koan Mu:

> For many years questioning the Mu of Joshu.
> Doubts coming and going, crossing between being and
>   nothingness.
> A mountain of silver, a wall of iron, forgetting myself.
> With all my being, one great shout of Mu.

This verse is easy to understand. The writer here took about six years "questioning the Mu of Joshu." "Questioning" means doubting, becoming a great mass of doubt.

"Doubts coming and going, crossing between being and nothingness." "Doubts" in this case are not doubts in the usual sense. Rather, it means that the great mass of doubt has become deeper and deeper. "Being and nothingness" refers to the dualistic view of understanding and not understanding, is and is not.

The third line, "A mountain of silver, a wall of iron, forgetting myself" is most important. "A mountain of silver, a wall of iron" is a great obstruction, something that cannot be broken down easily. The phrase refers to that which confronts us or stands in the way of our practice.

"Forgetting myself" means to be one with the silver mountain, the iron wall. When we come up against a hard wall, inevitably we want to use some means to break it down. With a hammer and chisel, we try to break down this mountain or wall. But as long as we employ some means or strategy, we will never be able to destroy it. What should you do? You must become the silver mountain, the iron wall itself. Forget the self by absorbing yourself in zazen. There is no other way to break down this "mountain of silver" or this "wall of iron."

In the final line, "With all my being" means the whole body from the top of your head to the tips of your toes. The whole body doesn't refer only to one person—it means together with all things: mountains, rivers, grasses, and trees. "One great shout of Mu" means to disgorge, to vomit up, to expel with the whole body, together with all things, one great shout of Mu.

This example of Mu is similar to other methods of zazen. Whether it is shikantaza, following the breath, counting breaths, or koan practice, these are all essentially the same. Don't think of it as applying only to Mu. This verse applies to all forms of zazen.

Please don't use small tricks or devices to try to break down this mountainous wall. Instead, I would like you to be completely a samadhi of zazen. This is certainly something you can do, so please *make the effort to thoroughly be* your practice, *to be* your zazen.

The contents of enlightenment, the actual condition of liberation, or, as in the verse I just mentioned, the condition where all becomes *Mu*, these are conditions that you cannot reach by means of thought, no matter how much you think about them or how much knowledge you have. You cannot even see them in a dream. Don't do your practice imagining these things. Let them all go, and each of you simply be one with your own zazen.

Completely be the cause. Since cause and result are one, you won't need to search for the result. The result is already manifested. Please don't practice zazen *within* your imaginings or expectations of the result. This would be "seeking mind." I would like you only to completely, totally, and purely make the effort to be the cause.

Expressing this in another way, the various kinds of zazen practice that we use to forget the self are like a walking stick that we use temporarily. I would like you to rely on this stick completely. Since you cannot do this all the time, sometimes you forget it, and sometimes it is bothersome, and for those reasons the ego-self does not fall away.

"Every person is amply endowed with the Dharma, but without practice it will not be manifested, without enlightenment it will not be attained." These are Zen Master Dogen's words. "The Dharma" is the condition as-it-is right now. It is your reality. "Each person" refers to people who have deep zazen experience as well as to those who have never done zazen. Each person is fully and amply endowed with the Dharma. "Without practice it will not be manifested" means that even if you are amply endowed with the Dharma, if you do not practice zazen, the activity of the Dharma will not appear. With regard to zazen practice, when you do zazen single-mindedly without mixing in your own ideas and just abandon yourself to zazen, then the body and mind will naturally be cast off.

With regard to both the outer form and the inner principle, I think you already understand the significance of zazen well enough. All you have to do is practice. To practice means, as we say in Japanese, "to break your bones," or to make a great effort. By persevering in "*breaking your bones*," you can attain the Way.

Shakyamuni Buddha said that anyone can attain the Dharma. He used the following metaphor to explain this: "Holding this stick, hitting the earth." If you throw a stick you are holding down toward the ground, it will be absolutely impossible to miss hitting the ground. Similarly, if you persevere with zazen, liberation will be as certain as the stick that cannot miss hitting the ground. Anyone can attain liberation.

Fundamentally, it is because of attachment to the ego-self that you have forgotten that you have your essence in your pocket. Delusion is the condition of desperately looking for it. Essentially, the Dharma is yours. So if you practice correctly and look for it, surely you can get hold of it.

Sit single-mindedly. Penetrate zazen.

■ REPENTANCE

In the belief in, study, and practice of Buddhism, the fundamental touchstone is repentance. Buddhist practice begins with repentance. You may have noticed in what I've said so far that the teaching of Buddhism is mostly saving oneself by oneself. It isn't a matter of relying on so-called gods and buddhas in order to be saved. In Zen it is the essence of repentance that is practiced. In other religions, repentance is the act of confessing your misdeeds. You go to an appropriate place and confess your sins. But the other type of repentance, the one of principle, or essence, is zazen. And that is what we are doing right now.

The following section from the *Sutra of Fugen (Samantabhadra) Bodhisattva* deals with the nature of repentance in Buddhism:

> The ocean of all karmic hindrance arises completely from delusion. If you wish to repent, then sit and think of the true nature of reality. All faults and bad deeds will vanish like frost and dew. All darkness will disappear in the light of wisdom.

If you want to repent, then do zazen and ascertain the essence of things. All faults and misdeeds, big and small, that you have knowingly committed will disappear just as frost and dew vanish in sunlight. "All darkness will disappear in the light of wisdom." This means that the light of wisdom achieved through zazen will make the darkness of delusion disappear completely.

As I've often said, zazen itself is the true form of reality. In other words, it is formless. There is no room in zazen for the ego-self or "me" to intervene. By means of zazen, that is to say, if zazen becomes zazen, then all faults and bad deeds will disappear immediately. To show how repentance is fulfilled simply by sitting in zazen, we chant the following "Verse of Repentance":

> All our past evil deeds were
> The result of beginningless greed, anger, and ignorance,
> Products of our body, speech, and thought.
> I now repent of all these deeds.

In the first line is the word "past." Understand the past as one second ago, one hour ago, ten years ago, thirty years ago, as well as the "beginningless" beginning, or "before your father and mother were born."

One thing I would like to point out to you is how "evil deeds" are understood in Buddhism. Various hindrances and obstacles arise and keep us from realizing our goal of attaining the Way. We want to practice, but because we are distracted by circumstances we cannot. In Buddhism, the conditions that prevent us from practicing are what we call "bad" or "evil."

I spoke just now from the standpoint of Buddhism, but it is the same in our ordinary life as well. There are those in the everyday world whose life is the Way, even though they have never once practiced zazen. What is considered bad or evil in the world is, of course, included in the Buddhist meaning of bad or evil.

In the second line of this verse, "the result of beginningless greed, anger, and ignorance," the word "beginningless" refers to a period spanning a beginningless beginning to an end without end. Due to the evil deeds brought about since a beginningless beginning by greed, anger, and ignorance, attainment of the Way is difficult.

The present result of not having attained the Way has for each of us been brought about by causes in the past that have led to our present condition. The present result will be a cause in the future. The result is a cause and that will be the future. This means that if you haven't attained it now, it is clear you won't in the future, either. Since there is only a continuation of moments "now," as long as we cannot accept our condition as-it-is, we will forever be seeking something somewhere else and for that reason will never be able to reach it.

The third line follows from the second. Evil deeds arise from greed, anger, and ignorance. From where did greed, anger, and ignorance arise? They are "products [created from] our body, speech, and thought." In the last line, "I now repent of all these deeds" means that "I, together with all things," now make repentance. "Together with all things" is important. When Shakyamuni Buddha attained liberation, he said, "Together with all things sentient and insentient the Way has been attained." That is why, in the same way, when we repent individually, it is done "together with all things sentient and insentient."

This is the way, then, that repentance is explained in words. But zazen itself is the way to express the complete repentance of the body, speech, and thought in actuality. This is the condition in which the perception of "I" or "me" brought about by the consciousness of the ego-self has vanished like frost and dew. This is what we call "the true form of repentance." Since it is the true form, it is the formless essence of things. From the principle that "true form is no form," it is only natural that the condition where one person repents must be one of thorough repentance done together with all sentient and insentient things.

"Buddha-mind, the Mind of Great Compassion" refers to the Buddha's great compassionate mind, which is the functioning of our mind in total repentance. That is why I always say that the end point of practice is not the condition of oneness or complete enlightenment, or forgetting the self, or the verification of liberation. It often happens that it is easy to think of the conclusion of Buddhist practice as realizing oneness, forgetting the self, or being enlightened. In fact, though, the teaching is that the point we thought was the end is actually the place where practice begins. This is what is usually referred to as "nothing to realize, nothing to attain." This is where all practice begins by means of the condition of No-Self. This is what we call the Way of Buddha.

This may sound theoretical, but as long as there is someone believing in something, in effect that means the ego-self or "I" is that "someone" that believes. In other words, repentance is not complete, and for that reason belief is not the true meaning of belief. It may seem as if we can truly believe, but as long as "I" remains, our belief will falter when we meet certain conditions. This is because repentance has not truly been exhausted. Belief is the result of not having totally repented.

To give a simple example, when you think to yourself, "I did something bad," at that instant repentance is complete. I would like you to fix this firmly in your mind. Thus, it is possible to forget the ego-self only by coming in contact with some condition or circumstance. "I did something bad." That itself is sufficient. It is the condition of total repentance.

In the context of zazen, this means that when the thought arises, "Today I'm really going to make an effort. I've got to start right now. I'm going to sit single-mindedly," you are already one with zazen. Nevertheless, at the very instant you think of good or bad deeds, right away the ego-self jumps in. "I did something bad, but . . ." This is the functioning of the ego-self. "I have to do it, but . . ." This thought arises the next instant. I would like you to understand it is to this degree that the appearance and disappearance, the life and death, of the ego-self is intense and unrelenting.

ZEN AND THE PRECEPTS ARE ONE

I would like to add one or two things to what I have said about repentance. In simple terms, I think we can understand the precepts as tenets of Buddhist morality. What must be followed or observed is that we must not add our own ideas to the condition right now. In other words, there must be no intervention of the ego-self. This is what must be maintained.

Some people are taught, and consequently think, that in order to "grind up" the ego-self consciousness it is enough simply to sit in zazen. This is equivalent to viewing the forty-nine years of Shakyamuni Buddha's teachings, the 84,000 gates of the Dharma, through the small window of Zen. "Simply sit. All will be resolved if you sit." This is to peek at Buddhism through a small opening. When viewing Zen from the larger standpoint of Buddhism, there must be the teaching that Zen and the precepts are one. Essentially it is impossible to have Zen without the precepts. At the same time there is no Buddhism in which there are only precepts and no Zen.

For example, Zen corresponds to oneness, or the absolute. The precepts correspond to difference, or the relative. It is comparatively easy to clarify the wisdom of equality, or the absolute. This is wisdom attained through the enlightenment of Zen. "I'm enlightened. All is empty." This kind of wisdom is easy to realize and attain through zazen. However, the wisdom of difference—in Sanskrit, *patimokkha*, "the liberation of each individual thing"—is said to be very difficult to clarify.

In general, this is, as I said earlier, zazen of the body, speech, and thought. These three aspects correspond with our bodily actions, our words, and our thoughts. These three aspects are Zen; they are zazen. Please don't simply think that everything will be resolved by sitting. I would like all of you who plan to continue with zazen to understand that the contents of sitting must be the precepts. In other words, zazen and the precepts are one. This is something you must understand. Zen and the precepts are one thing. If either is missing, it is not true Zen.

However, it isn't a matter of observing the sixteen precepts one by one. Some people are mistaken in thinking that if they follow the precepts faithfully and strictly, they will then forget the self, attain liberation, and clarify buddha-nature. Simply following the precepts or making others follow them is like putting a snake inside a length of bamboo. As the bones of a snake are soft, its essential nature is to bend back and forth when it moves. Inside a bamboo, its movements are very restricted so it stretches itself out straight. As soon as it gets out of the bamboo, though, it will return right away to its natural way of moving from side to side. Observing the precepts, being familiar with them, is entirely different from the condition of a snake in a length of bamboo.

Essentially, human beings cannot live life bound by morality, religious ethics, and all the other restrictions of society. People are fundamentally free of such bonds and fetters. By sitting for six years, Shakyamuni learned from the laws of nature that man is not bound or restricted. This was not something he created or invented. This was the law of causation. We are now sitting in zazen and making an effort to extinguish the ego-self. This liberation is not something learned from someone else. By doing zazen we are putting an end to the ego-self by becoming one with this natural principle. We are practicing in order to be one with this law of nature.

MIND CANNOT BE GRASPED

There is an expression in the Diamond Sutra that "the three worlds of mind cannot be grasped." "The three worlds of mind" are the mind of the past, the mind of the present, and the mind of the future.

Concerning the following story, it isn't good to think, "Oh, yes. That's how it is, isn't it?" as if it were someone else's problem. I would rather like you to think, "If that's the way it is, surely it's possible for me to become like this, too." Please have this kind of confidence.

The following anecdote originates from China. In the southern part of that country, a Zen priest by the name of Ryutan was teaching that "the mind itself is Buddha." This has the same meaning as "every-day mind is the Way."

One day, Tokusan, a scholar of the Diamond Sutra, heard of Ryutan's teaching and set out to convert him, in other words, humiliate him. The reason Tokusan felt it necessary to go and convert Ryutan was that in the sutra it was written that in order to become a buddha, it was necessary to practice for several lifetimes. Thus, Tokusan thought it absurd that Ryutan was teaching "the mind itself is Buddha." This, he felt, could only serve to sow great confusion among people who heard this, which is why he set off to reform Ryutan.

Tokusan took along his many treatises on the Diamond Sutra. Before reaching the gate leading into Ryutan's temple, he passed a small tea shop that served snacks and tea. As it was around noon, Tokusan entered the shop and ordered some rice cakes. He was served by the owner, an old woman. After exchanging pleasantries, their talk turned to Tokusan's reason for coming. "I am Tokusan, a scholar of the Diamond Sutra. I have heard that Ryutan is teaching that 'the mind itself is Buddha,' which, in my opinion, is outrageous. I am now going to do Dharma battle with him and change his mind. I have come all this way to convert him."

The woman set the plate of rice cakes in front of Tokusan and their dialogue began. The woman said, "You say you are a scholar of the Diamond Sutra. Lately, I have spoken with Priest Ryutan concerning this sutra. Is it true that in this sutra are the words, 'The mind of the past is ungraspable, the mind of the present is ungraspable, and the mind of the future is ungraspable'?" Tokusan replied, "That is true. The mind of the past, present, or future cannot be grasped. Essentially, the mind cannot be perceived. All delusion arises because of the mistake in thinking that the mind lies somewhere within the body." Tokusan proudly answered the woman in this way and then added, "Many people think—and it is taught this way in many religions—that the mind is the foundation that must be polished, and that peace of mind is achieved by disciplining the mind. They think this is surely the way to become a fine person."

On hearing this, the old woman asked, "You've just entered this shop and asked for a snack. I've brought the rice cakes you ordered. But I would like to ask you one thing. If the three worlds of mind—past, present, and future—are impossible to grasp, with which mind will you eat the rice cakes?"

Tokusan was dumbfounded by this question. He thought, "Surely, as it is written, the mind of the past, the mind of the present, and the mind of the future cannot be grasped. Certainly, in order to satisfy the mind, to relieve my hunger, I've asked for a snack. But if the mind does not exist in any of the three worlds of time, then why do I want to satisfy it? Where is the mind that can be gratified and that must be satisfied?" This is what Tokusan realized. Up until then he understood well the meaning of the words, but when he was actually asked about them he couldn't answer. From embarrassment, perspiration flowed down his forehead and he was sweating under his arms.

In the dialogue, Tokusan had tripped. He could not answer, and became greatly embarrassed. The wonderful thing about him is that he was able to bring it back to himself by making this problem his own. At this time he was not yet a Zen priest. There can be no doubt that he had taken a lot of time and trouble to study the Diamond Sutra. And yet with this one question, "Where is the mind?" he realized that all his study was worthless. This is truly wonderful.

After that he went to see Ryutan. While engaged in discussion, that is to say, doing Dharma battle, it grew dark. To show Tokusan to the door, Ryutan used a lamp. This was the old-fashioned style of lamp, consisting of a candle inside a paper lantern. Ryutan bent over to illuminate the entryway so that Tokusan could see his shoes. Just at the instant Tokusan was about to put on his shoes, Ryutan blew out the candle and at once it became pitch dark. At that moment, Tokusan attained enlightenment.

There can be no doubt that from the time of his dialogue with the old woman in the tea shop until his meeting with Ryutan, Tokusan was truly perplexed and filled with shame. His condition "ripened." The instant the light was blown out was the circumstance that brought about his enlightenment.

The next day Tokusan took into the garden all the treatises he had brought with him, the writings he had labored over for so long, and burned them. He then became a Zen monk and a disciple of Ryutan. Throughout his teaching life, Tokusan taught the Dharma with the pronouncement, "Thirty blows if you speak, thirty blows if you don't." If you could speak, he would hit you thirty times with the kyosaku stick. If you remained silent, he would also hit you thirty times. This was his method of teaching.

Imagine if Tokusan suddenly appeared in front of you now and asked, "What is zazen?" or "What is the Way?" or "What is sesshin?" If we said, "Zazen is such and such," or "the Way is so and so," and answered Tokusan in this way, thirty blows would come flying at us. How could we answer Tokusan so that he would agree and say, "That's right"? That is the problem.

My request is that you all become big people who can snatch Tokusan's kyosaku stick and beat him with it. Make a great effort. Give it all you have.

THE ENLIGHTENMENT OF GENSHA

I think many people find a Zen retreat difficult because of the pain in your legs. In light of this, I would like to return to the story of

Gensha, the monk who trained under the Zen master Seppo and was enlightened through pain.

For more than ten years Gensha had practiced intensely in the monastery. However, he couldn't seem to make the one last step needed for a resolution, so he decided to go to another place to practice. He stole away from the monastery in the dark of night. Since the path leading down the mountain was a rough one, Gensha had to tread carefully to avoid the rocks and tree stumps.

Gensha was concentrating so hard on picking his way down the mountain path that he totally forgot himself. His only concern as he walked was not to stumble and injure himself. And yet he did. He stubbed his toe on a rock, tearing off a toenail. This was extremely painful. "Ouch!" he yelled. First arose the thought, "It hurts." The next thought that followed closely was, "From where does this pain arise? My master, Seppo, always says that the body does not exist. From where, then, does the pain come?"

At that moment, by means of this conscious thought, Gensha was able to bring a resolution to his practice of zazen, which he had worked at for so long. Body and mind had fallen away. With the arising of this conscious thought, "From where does this pain come?" he had completely forgotten the ego-self. It was no longer necessary for Gensha to go to another place to practice, so he returned to Seppo.

Gensha descended this rocky mountain path in the dark taking the utmost care. His only concern was not to be careless and hurt himself. By means of that careful attention he completely forgot the ego-self. First, there was the pain in the midst of No-Self. Then, there was the consciousness of pain in the midst of No-Self. This was the condition that brought about the complete resolution to his long-held doubt.

I would like each of you to absorb yourself in your practice to such an extent that you forget the self with the same care and caution that Gensha took as he descended the mountain in the dark. Do your practice with your whole body and soul. If you do it this way, the condition that will bring about enlightenment will surely appear.

The care that Gensha took not to be careless while walking is the same condition that each of you finds yourself in while working. This is zazen in movement. I would like you to have the confidence that if you do your work—whether you are sitting or not—as carefully as Gensha walked down the mountain that night, you will meet the condition necessary for enlightenment.

The following words are a well-known Zen expression: "Take a step off a hundred-meter pole and the true Self will be revealed throughout the ten directions." This refers to someone sitting on top of a very high pole. Take one step off the pole and the true Self will become as wide as the universe.

Regardless of whether you have been doing zazen for a long time or whether today is your first attempt, all of you are now sitting on top of this hundred-meter-high pole. For some reason, though, you cannot take this one step. You are afraid, or have some sort of attachment, or you are in love with yourself. In any case, you are stuck on top of the pole. But if, through the power of your zazen, you take one step off it, the true Self will appear throughout the ten directions. A truly great thing will be attained. This means that there will be a time when you will realize that each and everything is you. Please persist in your practice.

ZEN WITHIN MOVEMENT, ZEN WITHIN STILLNESS

On retreat, we emphasize Zen within stillness. Yet when we return home, it will be necessary to emphasize "zazen within movement."

At the end of each sesshin held at my temple in Japan, I say to those who are going home, "When you go back, please forget everything about the monastery, the Buddha, the Dharma, and Zen." Writing with a pen, painting with a brush, teaching students with blackboard and chalk—the work you do in your everyday life is already Zen. This means that if in your work and daily life you try to use what you have heard here or the knowledge of Zen you have gained by listening to a teacher, this will result in "putting another head on top of the one you already have." It is enough simply to put your whole body and mind into your work. In that way, by absorbing yourself and forgetting yourself, you are in samadhi. This is Zen within movement. If you consciously think, "This is Zen," or "I must be one with this," then that is not Zen within movement.

It is a curious thing, but most people who have attained enlightenment in the past have done so in Zen within movement. Why is this so? It is because in Zen within stillness, little by little without knowing it, we become attached to sitting.

However, even with regard to Zen within movement, there is a mistake that is easily made. Some people assume that the condition of being twisted and turned about by things is enlightenment because there is no self. The state of true liberation is one in which both the ego-self and other objects disappear. This is what we call "the emptiness of the Dharma, the emptiness of the ego-self." In the condition that I just spoke about, where the ego-self has disappeared but other things still exist, the Dharma remains. In such a condition it is only natural that there will be a return to the former condition where the ego-self exists.

This refers mainly to Zen within movement. For homemakers, this is work around the house, such as cooking, washing dishes, cleaning the house, doing the laundry, and so on. To throw your body and mind into these things and really do them with all your might is the practice of Zen. There are some people who think that practicing zazen is more important and valuable, and who look down on cooking and cleaning. But I would like you to realize that this way of thinking is greatly mistaken. On hearing this, there will be some who will think, "If sitting and moving are both Zen, then when I'm sitting and my legs begin to hurt I prefer to stand up and move around."

In this way, they become negligent about practicing zazen. Please be aware that this is clearly a case where a person has unknowingly become attached to Zen within movement.

In the same way, it is possible to become attached to practicing zazen without being aware of it. I have said enough about Zen in stillness so I think you understand. Nevertheless, there are some people who do not feel settled unless they are sitting. This is a condition in which a person is still not free. He or she is bound by a rope that cannot be seen.

BEING ATTACHED TO THE EGO-SELF

By perceiving the ego-self, conflict, disagreement, and disharmony are also perceived. For that reason it isn't possible to live peacefully. In that connection I would like to ask each of you, "Where is the ego-self?" If you look over your body from the top of your head to the tips of your toes, you will not find it. Our condition, then, is one where something that essentially does not exist is perceived to exist. This is why we suffer.

When you shut your eyes, it becomes dark. When you open your eyes, at once, without the least separation, things are visible. We wouldn't be able to see anything if there were a division between subject and object. Using the example of the function of sight, simply see as-it-is. In other words, this is the condition where it is impossible to perceive "me" or "I."

The greatest gap, or separation, is the one between "life" and "death." Normally, we are not aware of this, even though it is something that we must naturally feel. Usually we view "life" and "death" as two different realities. We are negligent of death in that we don't even think of the time when it will come. Although it is difficult to imagine, I could easily pass away at any moment, even as I am talking.

In Buddhism, we say life and death is the appearance of a thought and the disappearance of that thought. Appearing and disappearing, appearing and disappearing, thoughts coming and going—this is what we call "life and death." When one thought appears, we say "life"; when the thought disappears, we say "death." This means that we are always freshly born, and our life is always new and fresh. But in between life and death, in between two thoughts, we set up the ego-self. Then, because we see both life and death, the viewpoint of the ego-self arises so that we are happy with life and hate death. We are shaken by this. This is nothing more than a viewpoint of the ego-self.

When the ego-self that perceives life and death has completely disappeared, we say this is a condition where life and death are one. This means that the time of life is its Dharma condition as-it-is, and the time of death is its Dharma condition as-it-is. When the self has completely disappeared, the bonds of life and death are completely cut so great freedom is attained. This is called liberation, or the "body and mind cast off."

In our everyday life, if we think through any problem, no matter how small, we will certainly come up against life and death. If this problem of life and death can be resolved, all other problems will be resolved simultaneously. You will be able to concentrate fully on your work, your efficiency will rise, and you will be able to live your life in freedom.

Zen practice resolves the problem of life and death. Our practice is to kill that self by means of the power of zazen. "To kill" is a strong expression, but it is not only killing the self; at the same time it is dying with all things. Since it is to die together with all things, this is not something sad or lonely or full of suffering. This is what we call "dying the Great Death."

"Dying the Great Death" is a condition where all has been extinguished, all has disappeared, where there is not one thing alive. As there is nothing to compare, it is very peaceful and comfortable. There is no longer any need to be deluded. This is the condition of being free of life and death.

In contrast to this is living. This is being together with all things. There is no death or disappearance. For that reason it isn't possible to compare life and death. It is only each thing, each activity, so there is peace of mind. This is what we call "the Great Activity appears."

Through the condition of our father and mother coming together, the moon became full and we were born. It is impossible to remember your own birth. At the same time it isn't possible to be aware of your own death. Normally, we say a person has been born and a person has died, but this is nothing but the viewpoint of the ego-self, from which arises the problem of life and death. People usually think their life starts with birth and ends with death, but this isn't the reality. It is nothing but the life of the ego-self. To realize that there is an essential Self that does not undergo birth and death and then look for it is Zen practice. This is the Way of Buddha and must be the goal of human life.

As I have said repeatedly, as long as you do not find the true Self and make it your own, no matter how satisfying your life may seem, there will always remain a feeling of loneliness or a feeling that something is lacking. To explain this in a way that is easy to understand, delusion is usually explained as the separation between self and things. In fact, however, delusion is the fight between the true Self and the ego-self. It is the entanglements and conflict of the ego-self.

Please don't be twisted and turned about by things. I would like you to grasp the true, essential Self.

In the Lotus Sutra are the following words: "Seek the real Self with an adoring, loving mind; with a thirsty, longing mind." With this attitude please seek the true Self. Buddhist practice must be done reflecting the same attitude as being in love. I would like you to search for the true Self with a loving, longing mind.

▌ LIBERATION IS LEAVING THE DHARMA AS-IT-IS

There is a famous dialogue between a master and his disciple that I would like to relate.

One day Kyozan asked his master Isan, "What would happen if all things arose at the same time?" "All things" refers to myriad things or phenomena. It is everything that a human being can imagine. "If all such things were to arise at once, what should I do?"

I think each of you encounters this situation everyday. The question is: "What is the best way to resolve this?" Isan answered him by saying, "Yellow is not blue, long is not short. Leaving all aspects of the Dharma as-they-are, they don't concern me." This means, in short, that it is best to leave things as they are. "Leave all aspects of the Dharma as-they-are" is to leave each thing in its place. This is differentiation as-it-is. This is suffering as-it-is, enjoyment as-it-is, sadness as-it-is, joyfulness as-it-is. This is the liberation of leaving things as-they-are.

Another way that the words "they don't concern me" can be explained is in connection with the ego-self, of which I have often spoken. This is all things as-they-are. It is self and object as one. It is where there is no space for the ego-self to intervene. "Leave all aspects of the Dharma as-they-are" also means no ego-self and only the Dharma.

We are now practicing zazen. While sitting, various thoughts arise: at times discrimination, at times delusion or random thoughts, at times complications of the ego-self, and many others. These movements of the mind are also objects. If objects are left as-they-are, there is no ego-self. This flowing stream of many, many thoughts is the Dharma itself, as-it-is. There is absolutely no room for the intervention of the ego-self.

"The sitting today went relatively well," or "the sitting today was really difficult." These conditions are the Dharma, the place of the Dharma. "Leaving all aspects of the Dharma as-they-are, they don't concern me." It is necessary in this way to develop the power to leave things as-they-are, whether they are favorable or unfavorable, pleasant or unpleasant.

The source of the consciousness of the ego-self is called the "store consciousness" (Skt.: *alaya-vijnana*). This consciousness is said to be the origin of delusion. It is said that we seek "to measure the self that is No-Self." Even though it is impossible to perceive "me" or the ego-self in the slightest degree, we try to measure and set a value on the self. We assume there is a self. This is the sickness of perception. The biggest sickness is that we delude ourselves by perceiving the self.

DEAD OR ALIVE?

I would like to pose a question for you to consider.

One day a disciple accompanied his master to a funeral. Pointing to the body in the coffin, the disciple asked, "Is it dead or alive?"

The master replied, "I won't say if it's dead and I won't say if it's alive."

"Why don't you answer?" the disciple asked.

The master's reply was, "I won't say. I won't say."

On the way home from the funeral, as the problem of life and death lay heavy on the disciple's mind, he asked the question again. "Is it dead or alive?"

Again the master answered, "I won't say if it's dead and I won't say if it's alive."

The disciple said, "If you don't answer me, I'll hit you. Please tell me, is it dead or alive?"

The master's reply was, "I won't say. I won't say."

I would like you now to be the master in this story. If you were asked, "Is it dead or is it alive?" what would you say? This is the problem I pose for you. It is Tokusan's "thirty blows if you speak, thirty blows if you don't." This dialogue between disciple and master captures the problem of life and death for you. This isn't someone else's problem. It is your own problem. Please consider it well.

The Chinese character for *Dharma* is written with the components of "water" and "to leave." As this character implies, water flows naturally from a high place to a low place. It means to experience the Truth, which is separate from the judgment and intervention of the ego-self. In other words, if you really know yourself, then you can use the world as a basis to decide what you want to do.

As I have said in the text, in our lifetime there is only one person we must encounter, one person we must meet as though we were passionately in love. That person is the essential Self, the true Self. As long as you don't meet this Self, it will be impossible to find true satisfaction in your heart, to avoid feeling that you lack something, or to be clear about things in general.

To meet your Self is said to be the purpose of human life. It is also the objective in Buddhism. The shortest, most practical way to do this is through Zen. Buddhism is the teaching of the Dharma, which Shakyamuni Buddha expounded after his liberation. This was not a conclusion he arrived at within the realm of ego-self thought, whereby reality is perceived as objective and thought is used to determine what reality is. Rather, Buddha discovered the nature of reality by liberating himself from discriminatory, dualistic thought and became reality itself. For that reason, his teaching of present reality is far different from the sort of explanation of reality that depends on knowing and not knowing (dualistic thought), which is generally prevalent in the fields of religion, philosophy, physics, medicine, and biology.

The reality that Shakyamuni Buddha revealed was reality itself, the nature of completely assimilated reality, which is what we refer to as "the Dharma." The teaching that Buddha expounded was that the existence of things with and without form is separate from human thought. All things appear because of conditions, and all things disappear because of conditions. The appearance and disappearance of things has absolutely no connection with the ego-self. As all things are formed through conditions, they have no center or substance. For that reason, things are constantly changing (are impermanent), have no beginning and end (are selfless), and cannot be perceived (are formless).

The Dharma (present reality) is separate from human thought. Thus people mistakenly assume that what they think and perceive is reality. In this way, people create "a fantasy" by thinking that something that cannot be perceived is reality. Attachment to this delusion and chasing after it result in various sufferings. To be deluded by the sufferings of birth, old age, sickness, and death is not to be deluded by these realities but rather to be deluded *within the thought of the ego-self*. Birth, old age, sickness, and death are also the Dharma as it is apart from the thought of the ego-self. Measuring the realm of causality—which is birth, old age, sickness, and death—by the standard of dualistic thought of the ego-self is why problems such as suffering arise.

The Dharma of birth, old age, sickness, and death has absolutely no relation to the ego-self. They appear and disappear, appear and disappear, and that's the end of it. If you are one with conditions, there is absolutely no need for resolution. The reason we lack complete confidence that we can arrive at a resolution to the problem of life and death is that we blindly believe in causality and, at the same time, we approve of our own way of thinking. We understand that present reality appears because of causality, but because of the weakness of our belief in causality being separate from the thought of the ego-self, our habit of measuring the present condition with standards of the ego-self remains and does not disappear.

The path expounded by Buddha is simply to accept birth, old age, sickness, and death as your own reality and not to interfere with that reality by using the thought of the ego-self. It is my hope that the material in this book, taken as a whole, can be the "condition" to allow as many people as possible to encounter their true Self.

■■ ZEN MASTERS AND MONKS APPEARING IN THE TEXT

CHINESE MASTERS

(citations are alphabatized by the Japanese pronunciation and spelling; Chinese spellings appear in parenthesis)

Baso	(Mazu; 709–88)
Bodai Daruma	(Bodhidharma; d. 532)
Daie	(Dahui; 1089–1163)
Daikan Eno	(Dajian Huineng; 638–713)
Daiman Konin	(Daman Hongren; 601–74)
Gensha	(Xuansha; 9th century)
Hotetsu	(Baoche; 9th century)
Hyakujo	(Baizhang; 749–814)
Isan	(Guishan; 771–853)
Jinshu	(Shenxiu; d. 706)
Joshu	(Zhaozhou; 778–897)
Kanchi Sosan	(Jianzhi Sengcan; d. 606?)
Kyogen	(Xiangyan; d. 898)
Kyozan	(Yangshan; 807–83 or 813–90)
Mumon	(Wumen; 1183–1260)
Nansen Fugan	(Nanquan Puyuan; 748–835)
Rinzai	(Linji; d. 866)
Ryutan	(Longtan; 9th century)

Sekito Kisen	(Shitou Xiqian; 700–790)
Sekkyo	(Shigue; 9th century)
Seppo	(Xuefeng; 822–908)
So Toba	(Su Tungpo; 1036–1101)
Taiso Eka	(Dazu Hulke; 487–593)
Tendo Nyojo	(Tiantong Rujing; 1163–1228)
Tokusan	(Deshan; 781–867)
Yakusan	(Yaoshan; 745–828)
Zuigan	(Ruiyan; 9th century)

JAPANESE MASTERS

Dogen	(1200–1253)
Kanzan	(1277–1360)
Ryokan	(1758–1831)

Buddhadharma. The teaching Shakyamuni Buddha expounded as a result of his awakening that the true nature of things is constantly changing (transient), without beginning or end (selfless), and cannot be perceived (formless).

Dharma. The provisional name given to the way things are as-they-are, i.e., mountains are high, rivers are low, sugar is sweet, salt is salty. Truth. It is also used synonymously with Buddhadharma.

Heart Sutra. One of the most important sutras in Mahayana Buddhism and particularly emphasized in Zen. It expounds in a clear and concise manner the teaching of emptiness.

Kensho. Directly seeing into one's true nature. Synonymous with satori.

Koan. Originally, a koan meant a legal case that set precedent as law, something that cannot be tampered with. The word is now used primarily to refer to: 1) the questioning mind; 2) stories and dialogues of Zen masters that are used as a method to help someone focus in the practice of Zen. In both cases, a koan is ultimate reality itself and is something that cannot be understood or not understood, defined, or given significance by means of human thought.

Kyosaku. A short stick used to rouse and encourage sitters in the *zendo.*

Roshi. Traditionally, a title given to an enlightened Zen master. However, in present-day Japan the standards are far less strict, and Zen priests are often addressed as "Roshi" merely out of respect for their position and age.

Samadhi. Complete absorption in the activity itself so that both oneself and the activity are forgotten.

Satori. Zen term for awakening, enlightenment.

Sesshin. A period of especially intense devotion to the practice of zazen from early in the morning until late at night. A sesshin typically lasts from two days to a week.

Shikan. Single-mindedly being the activity itself.

Shikantaza. Often translated as "just sitting" or "single-minded sitting." However, it has a much broader meaning. It is the practice of doing each activity in our life for the sake of that activity, regardless whether we are sitting, lying down, working, and so on.

Shoyoroku. *The Book of Serenity*, a collection of 100 koans compiled in the twelfth century by the Chinese Zen master Wanshi Shogaku (Hongzhi Zhengzhue; 1091–1157).

Skandhas. The five components that comprise body and mind: form, sensation, perception, formation, and consciousness.

Teisho. A presentation of the Dharma during sesshin by a Zen master in the form of a commentary on a koan or an important passage in Zen literature. A teisho is the immediate demonstration of his or her insight into the theme or material.

Tripitaka. The three sections of the Buddhist teachings: the precepts, the sutras, and the commentaries.

Zendo. A hall in which to practice zazen.

Zuisokkan. A method of zazen whereby a person temporarily relies on following the breath as an aid to becoming single-minded.

■■ ABOUT WISDOM PUBLICATIONS

Wisdom Publications, a nonprofit publisher, is dedicated to making available authentic works relating to Buddhism for the benefit of all. We publish books by ancient and modern masters in all traditions of Buddhism, translations of important texts, and original scholarship. Additionally, we offer books that explore East-West themes unfolding as traditional Buddhism encounters our modern culture in all its aspects. Our titles are published with the appreciation of Buddhism as a living philosophy, and with the special commitment to preserve and transmit important works from Buddhism's many traditions.

To learn more about Wisdom, or to browse books online, visit our website at www.wisdompubs.org.

You may request a copy of our catalog online or by writing to this address:

Wisdom Publications
199 Elm Street
Somerville, Massachusetts 02144 USA
Telephone: 617-776-7416
Fax: 617-776-7841
Email: info@wisdompubs.org
www.wisdompubs.org

THE WISDOM TRUST

As a nonprofit publisher, Wisdom is dedicated to the publication of Dharma books for the benefit of all sentient beings and dependent upon the kindness and generosity of sponsors in order to do so. If you would like to make a donation to Wisdom, you may do so through our website or our Somerville office. If you would like to help sponsor the publication of a book, please write or email us at the address above.

Thank you.

Wisdom is a nonprofit, charitable 501(c)(3) organization affiliated with the Foundation for the Preservation of the Mahayana Tradition (FPMT).

Opening the Hand of Thought
Foundations of Zen Buddhist Practice
Kosho Uchiyama * Foreword by Shohaku Okumura
Edited by Shohaku Okumura, Tom Wright, and Jisho Warner
256 pages, ISBN 0861713575, $16.95

"Uchiyama Roshi's words have long been my inspiration, and I am delighted that this collection of his teachings is now available in a revised and expanded edition."—Robert Aitken, author of *Taking the Path of Zen*

Sitting With Koans
Essential Writings on the Practice of Zen Koan Introspection
Edited by John Daido Loori * Introduction by Thomas Yuho Kirchner
352 pages, ISBN 0861713699, $16.95

"Required reading for those interested in how koans are used in Zen practice. For the practitioner, the real strength of this volume is the presentation of selected koans, with commentaries by authorized Japanese, Chinese, and American Rinzai Zen masters."—*Shambhala Sun*

The Art of Just Sitting
Essential Writings on the Zen Practice of Shikantaza
Edited by John Daido Loori
Foreword by Taigen Dan Leighton
256 pages, ISBN 086171394X, $16.95

"The single most comprehensive treasury of writings on the subject in English. This volume, spanning the centuries since Shakymuni Buddha to the present day, will prove indispensable to meditators and scholars alike. Roshi John Daido Loori has given us a rare treasure."—John Daishin Buksbazen, author of *Zen Meditation in Plain English*

How to Raise An Ox
Zen Practice as Taught in Master Dogen's Shobogenzo
Francis Dojun Cook * Foreword by Taizan Maezumi Roshi
208 pages, ISBN 0861713176, $14.95

"Simply the best, clearest, and most concise introduction to Dogen's Zen."—Barry Magid, author of *Ordinary Mind* and *Ending the Pursuit of Happiness*

Explore them all at wisdompubs.org.